Aviary Birds in Colour

AVIARY BIRDS IN COLOUR is exceptional among bird books for the magnificent quality of colour photographs by Dennis Avon and Tony Tilford. They are the fruit of high technical skill and long hours of painstaking work. Their excellence was widely acclaimed when they were featured in a major Kodak Exhibition in London. The selection of birds has been supervised by the Curator of Birds at the London Zoo, Mr Peter Olney, who has written the Foreword.

The text by Frank Woolham, former staffman with one of Britain's premier zoological gardens and an aviculturist for nearly thirty years, splendidly complements the colour photographs and gives a description of each species, general management, feeding and breeding.

Dennis Avon is a specialist in sophisticated colour printing methods and lectures in photography. Tony Tilford, a specialist in Educational Technology, is on the Council of the Royal Society for the Protection of Birds, and an active member of the British Trust for Ornithology.

At a time when conservation is the concern of many people, this book emphasises the contribution of the aviculturist in ensuring that wild bird species survive despite the many threats to their existence.

AVIARY BIRDS IN COLOUR is a worthy companion to Blandford's award-winning BIRDS OF BRITAIN AND EUROPE IN COLOUR, the standard two-volume HANDBOOK OF FOREIGN BIRDS, WILDFOWL OF THE WORLD, and many other bird books.

Aviary Birds in Colour

Photographed by
Dennis Avon & Tony Tilford

with text by
Frank Woolham

Blandford Press
Poole   Dorset

First published in Britain 1974
Reprinted 1979

Copyright © 1974 Blandford Press Ltd
Link House, West Street,
Poole, Dorset BH15 1LL

ISBN 0 7137 0707 0

ACKNOWLEDGEMENTS

The photographs in this book are the culmination of six years' work; specialist photography and the development of new techniques have consumed long hours and many weekends, and we must record most gratefully the forbearance and support of our wives, Wendy, May and Meg, in the preparation of this book. It would not have been possible without the invaluable help we have had from many other people, among whom we particularly mention the following:

Mr and Mrs M. Attew; Mr and Mrs K. Barnes (Nidus Bird Farm); Mr L. J. Boyce; Mr M. D. England; Mr R. Farrow; Mr A. Fielding; Mr I. Fraser; Mr J. Fraser; Mr A. Hawkins; Mr C. R. Hunt; Rt Hon. Lord Fisher and Mr and Mrs B. Dickson (Kilverstone New World Wildlife Park); Mr K. Lawrence; Mr K. Legget; Mr and Mrs H. E. Reynolds; Mr J. Roberts; Mr G. Shearing; Mr G. Smith (Attlebridge Pet Farm); Mr T. Taberham; Mr and Mrs T. Walker (Kelling Park Aviaries).

We would particularly like to thank Mr Peter Olney, Curator of Birds at the Zoological Gardens, Regent's Park, London, for the guidance he has given on the selection of species included in this book, and for writing the Foreword.

Dennis Avon

Tony Tilford

Frank Woodham

Printed and bound in Great Britain by
Fakenham Press Limited, Fakenham, Norfolk

Foreword

The use of birds by man dates back before written history. Symbolic figurines of pigeon-like birds have been found in northern Iraq which date from about 4500 BC. By 3000 BC, when written records first appeared, pigeons in Egypt had been domesticated for food and as message carriers. The domestic hen was part of the everyday scene in China and Egypt by 1400 BC, though it is likely they had been utilised long before then in the early civilisations of India. Birds may have been kept mainly as food, or in the case of hawks and cormorants, as food-hunters, but they have also been used for a variety of other purposes and have played a part in many aspects of human activity ranging from warfare to religious ritual. By Roman times birds figured prominently in paintings, sculptures, mosaics and in writings. They were used as objects of veneration, symbols of virtues and vices, as watchdogs, as sources of adornment, and significantly they were kept just for the pleasure and interest they provided. It is something of a paradox that they and other animals were also publicly slaughtered for the pleasure that that provided. However, it is obvious from the writings of such Romans as Pliny, Plutarch, Varro and Aelian that many species were kept as pets and that aviculture flourished. Parrots and peacocks from India, starlings, nightingales and finches were kept in private houses and parks much as they are today.

Aviculture has progressed since those days and many more species have shared man's abodes. Still the fundamental problem remains that if a man takes upon himself to be their guardian then he has a duty to look after them as well as he can. Often enough the avicultural information required does not seem to be available, and thoughtlessness or ignorance can lead to abuse or cruelty. There is a need for clear and concise information and this book, I think, provides just that. The author is to be congratulated on supplying the sort of detail that is always being asked for – details on accommodation, feeding, diseases, breeding and so on. Coupled with a description of each species are a series of quite outstanding photographs which not only identify the bird but will, in their own right, give great pleasure.

This is a book which I welcome, and which I know will be of considerable use. Like cookery books you need to use it over a period of time before you realise its full value.

P. J. Olney, Curator of Birds
Zoological Society of London

Contents

(For alphabetical Species Index see page 176)

Introduction

Aviculture is a hobby which has been carried on for centuries; birds of many species have been taken from the wild and acclimatised to aviary conditions. Now when we are aware of the many pressures inflicted by man on our wild creatures, we should be considering our hobby in a different light. Certain species are becoming rare, and others are likely to do so if birds are removed in large numbers from the wild. We cannot afford to keep birds in captivity for their beauty alone or even for seeking any competitive status.

More than ever before, all aviculturists should have a goal to aim for – the successful breeding of as many species as possible. Aviculture can no longer be merely an absorbing but aimless pastime. It is the responsibility of everyone who owns potential breeding birds, whether they be a few pairs of finches or a valuable collection of rare species, to ensure they are given every opportunity to nest and successfully raise young. The challenge is enormous, and the reward will be the satisfaction of knowing that one has succeeded in persuading a pair of wild creatures to accept an artificial, man-made environment to the extent that they are happy and confident enough to settle down and rear a family.

While studying birds in captivity the aviculturist can obtain information of considerable scientific value which may not be available from observations of birds in the wild. Recording of activity, display, feeding techniques, breeding etc., is an important role the aviculturist can play in conservation.

Initial expenditure will depend to a great extent on the kind of birds which make up the collection. Obviously an aviary to house some of the larger parrots is likely to cost a good deal more than one which will be occupied by a pair of small finches or softbills. Apart from the aviary itself there is not a great deal of basic equipment which needs to be purchased. Food and water vessels can be improvised – discarded plastic food containers are fine – some cages will be necessary to provide temporary accommodation for newly obtained birds, and a hospital cage is a valuable acquisition. Apart from the cost of the birds themselves, that is about the limit of necessary expenditure. Of course, the chances are that one's enthusiasm will flourish and the first small aviary will eventually be joined by others. No one can foresee the lengths to which a dedicated aviculturist will go in the pursuit of his hobby. One thing is certain: no matter what the expenditure, in terms of satisfaction and constant interest the return will far exceed it.

Accommodation As the title of this book implies, all the species described and illustrated are regarded as suitable subjects for outdoor aviaries or, in some cases, conservatories. For it is only in this more natural environment that regular breeding success is likely to be achieved. Cages have to be used from time to time. They are essential for newly imported birds which would quickly succumb if put outdoors, even during the summer months, as soon as they arrive. And there are other occasions – illness or accident, perhaps – when close confinement is essential. But we should regard cages as only temporary homes for any of the birds included in this book.

All too often a garden aviary ends up as a somewhat unlovely construction of wood or metal framing supporting a sagging sheet of wire-netting. Despite the most ingenious design ideas it is a little difficult to get away from this basic fact.

Fortunately, where the majority of aviary birds are concerned, it is not only possible but highly desirable to make use of growing plants in and around the finished structure. Not only

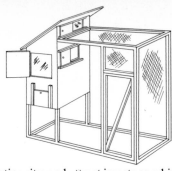

Fig. 1 Free-standing aviary

will they provide possible nesting sites and attract insects on which the birds will feed, but they can add considerably to the appearance of any aviary. It is not necessary to have an expert knowledge of horticulture to achieve all manner of delightful effects by the judicious use of various shrubs, herbaceous and climbing plants.

Aviaries can be either free-standing (Fig. 1) or built as lean-to structures against a convenient wall. There is much to be said for the latter arrangement if it is practical. A wall not only gives protection from the weather but also helps create an impression of greater seclusion and privacy for the occupants.

Whatever design is finally chosen, the size of the finished structure is usually governed by the amount of space available in the garden. There are no hard and fast rules as to maximum and minimum dimensions. Many people achieve excellent breeding results with a single pair of finches or small softbills housed in flights measuring about 2 m × 1 m × 2 m high (6 ft × 3 ft × 6 ft high). But it must be emphasised that such small aviaries are usually difficult to maintain in a planted state.

A minimum floor area of around 2·5 sq. m (27 sq. ft) allows much greater scope for attempts to create a natural environment. Normally, only one breeding pair of birds can be accommodated in these small units, but a slightly larger floor space allows the opportunity to introduce a pair of small quail or doves. These birds usually make good companions for even the most competitive breeding pairs of finches or small softbills.

Remember that a series of small-compartment aviaries will be of much more value than one large structure if serious attempts at breeding are contemplated. One disadvantage of these small flights is, of course, the provision of adequate shelter in each of them – a vital factor if the occupants are to remain outside throughout the year.

One solution is to build the flights on to a shed or birdroom and provide small connecting indoor flights (Fig. 2). This is a much less expensive proposition than building a separate shelter within each flight.

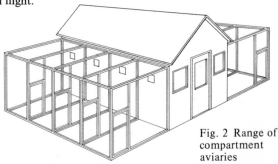

Fig. 2 Range of compartment aviaries

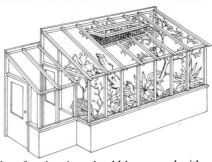

Fig. 3 Conservatory converted to an aviary

Part of the top and sides of each aviary should be covered with a rigid translucent plastic sheet. This provides some protection from driving winds and rain which, even during summer, can present a major hazard to many small birds.

Aviaries can be constructed by anyone with pretensions to being a handyman. Alternatively a number of firms will supply ready-made sectional aviaries which merely need to be erected on site and bolted together.

Greenhouses or conservatories can be adapted to provide excellent homes for certain soft-billed birds (Fig. 3). Humming birds, sunbirds and some small tanagers are among the species which thrive in the warm, humid conditions which can easily be created under glass. Essential modifications include roller-blinds (or green emulsion paint) to reduce light intensity through the roof-glazing, and plenty of ventilation with wire-netting covers for vents and windows.

Small conservatories are rarely practical as homes for birds. One of the biggest problems is to maintain a reasonably stable temperature. In a larger building there is no reason why, assuming some form of heating is employed, the birds should not be housed there throughout the year.

The most delicate or valuable hot-house plants will not be damaged by small nectar-feeding species provided the house is not overcrowded. In fact the plants are likely to derive considerable benefit since the birds will prove efficient at controlling insect pests.

While recognising that little successful breeding is likely to be achieved in the close confines of a cage, it is important that every aviculturist has one or two roomy stock cages to provide temporary accommodation for sick birds or newly obtained stock which need a period of quarantine and acclimatisation.

Cages of the box pattern are the only ones which are likely to be of much value. Ornamental wire cages are of little value; they offer no privacy and little protection from draughts and are not recommended for even brief occupation by any species.

A box cage (Fig. 4) measuring around 1 m × 500 mm × 400 mm (36 in. × 18 in. × 15 in.) can

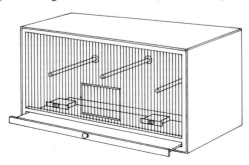

Fig. 4 Simple box cage

be used to house one or two small to medium-sized birds until they can be released into their permanent homes. Natural twig perches should be used if possible. The sliding drawer-tray can be covered with bird-sand (for hardbills) or sheets of old newspaper (for softbills). Wire fronts should *not* be of the type employed by canary breeders – that is with two or three circular bob-holes provided so that the occupants can reach external food and water vessels. These have been the cause of many a tragedy when pressed into service for wild species.

Every aviculturist should have a thermostatically-controlled hospital cage among his basic equipment. Several excellent models are on the market and if one has the misfortune to have a bird fall sick (something which could happen at any time) the special cage will prove invaluable, since heat and isolation are two important factors in effecting a cure.

Feeding A basic diet for the majority of small finches consists of a mixture of small plain canary seed, yellow and panicum millet; spray millet is added at regular intervals, and during late summer bunches of seeding grass-heads can be collected from the fields and hedgerows to supplement the staple diet.

Individual species may require additions. These are dealt with under the separate headings. But it is necessary to emphasise at this point that the contents of the seed dish should be regarded only as basic diet. Green food is essential for the vast majority of birds; a surprising number of finches require live food; even nectar mixtures and honey water will be consumed by the most unlikely species – once they are accustomed to them.

Sprouted seeds are an invaluable item of diet at all times, but particularly when there are youngsters to be reared. At this time, many seedeaters which have not required a great deal of live food become highly insectivorous until they have finished feeding their brood.

Grit and cuttlefish bone are essential at all times. Many aviculturists also make use of vitamin supplements, but in a well-planted and properly managed outdoor aviary most birds require little in the way of such additives. An imaginative approach to feeding a collection of seedeaters usually pays considerable dividends.

'Softbill' is an avicultural term used to describe birds which feed on insects, fruit, nectar, or a combination of these foods.

Some of the more insectivorous species are decidedly difficult to keep and should be obtained only by experienced aviculturists. With the exception of some of the bulbuls and the Pekin Robin, softbills are not birds for the beginner. They should not be considered until experience has been gained with a wide range of more easily managed seedeating species.

Most insectivorous softbills can be fed on one of the various prepacked insectile mixtures on the market. These are usually available in two grades – fine, for the smaller and more delicate species, and a coarser mixture which can be used for the bigger and more robust kinds. It is essential that this staple food is supplemented with as wide a variety of live food as possible. Mealworms and cleaned maggots are the most frequently used, especially in winter when there is little chance of collecting other items from the garden. Other types of live food which can be cultivated by the aviculturist include fruit flies (excellent for humming birds, sugarbirds, ixulus, etc.), locusts (fully grown they are an ideal food for starlings, jay-thrushes and some of the larger softbills; the young 'hoppers' can be fed to most of the smaller insectivorous species), blowflies – easily produced by allowing maggots to complete their life-cycle – various moths and beetles.

Many aviculturists prefer to make up their own insectile food; if the collection is large and comprehensive this is undoubtedly a good plan. But for the fancier with only a few pairs of softbills it makes more sense to use one of the proprietary mixtures. Opinions differ a great deal but many people add items ranging from raw meat to cheese to the prepared mixture;

others include finely chopped green food. Certainly there is much to be said for providing as varied a diet as possible, but the aviculturist must be careful not to overdo things with additives taken from the pantry or refrigerator. Feeding softbills is complex and it is virtually impossible to lay down hard and fast rules about specific diets for individual species. The fancier is strongly recommended to make a cautious approach, research his subject thoroughly and, wherever possible, take note of other people's experiences with similar species.

Fruit-eating softbills are not nearly as difficult to keep as the insectivorous species. Most of them will accept an appropriate grade of insectile food together with an assortment of fruits. Apples, pears, grapes, oranges and bananas are most frequently used. Bruised fruit is quite acceptable, but should never be fed in an overripe state. Oranges must be sweet; tomatoes are an excellent substitute.

Currants and sultanas soaked overnight can be fed to many species but the carbohydrate content is high and they should be used sparingly.

Many species of softbills are fond of berries: elderberries and blackberries can be gathered wild during late summer and autumn; raspberries and various currants as they are in season in the garden.

Nectar-feeding species include humming birds, sunbirds and some of the sugarbirds, zosterops and bananaquits. The last three will consume nectar in preference to other foods if given the chance, but this will have a detrimental effect on their health.

Humming birds are nowadays fed on a Gevral Protein and white-sugar mixture, which has produced excellent results in sustaining these beautiful little gems in good health over long periods. Fruit flies are an essential addition for most species.

Sunbirds can be fed on the same Gevral mixture but with a lower sugar content. Alternatively there are excellent nectar mixtures on the market which provide a good basic food for these birds. Again, fruit flies are an important item of diet for sunbirds. Small house flies, spiders, etc., can also be offered.

Although sugarbirds, zosterops and similar birds are frequently referred to as nectar feeders it is essential that they are given a rather more varied diet. A high-protein nectar is not necessary for these birds and they are better fed on a honey-and-water mixture – in which one can soak a piece of sponge cake. Fruit and live food should also be provided.

Diseases Always assuming birds are properly housed and fed, and that no undue risks are taken, most species are a good deal tougher than many people imagine. Sound management together with that indefinable, but essential, 'feel' for one's stock will do much to reduce the possibility of disease.

One of the most important factors in the successful treatment of a sick bird is the provision of heat. This can be achieved most effectively by use of a hospital cage. It is pointless putting the patient in a warm spot in the kitchen or dining-room where it will almost certainly be subjected to temperature fluctuations, particularly at night.

Quite often a bird suffering from a chill or some minor ailment will recover within a couple of days if hospitalised and kept at a constant temperature of 30 °C (85 °F). Naturally the temperature in the hospital cage must be reduced gradually to match that of the bird's normal environment before it is released again.

Modern antibiotics have proved of immense value in treating some of the more serious illnesses to which birds are subject. They are available through a veterinary surgeon's prescription. It is strongly recommended that professional advice is always sought – and quickly – when there is any uncertainty about the nature of a bird's illness.

Diagnosis is often difficult; in some cases it is impossible to ascertain the trouble except by post-mortem examination. But if you can provide the veterinary surgeon with brief but accurate details of the symptoms you have observed it may well assist in identifying the trouble.

The following are some of the more common problems which may be encountered – and treated – by the aviculturist.

Chills A cold or chill can prove fatal within a very short space of time unless steps are taken to combat the problem. The bird should be placed in a hospital cage for two or three days with the temperature set at 30 °C (85 °F). Recovery is usually swift. The early symptoms of an oncoming chill are not unlike those of the far more serious salmonellosis. In both cases the birds will appear dejected and lacking in energy; feathers are usually fluffed out, both feet grip the perch and there will be an increasing tendency to sleep.

Salmonellosis is usually fatal and if there are any doubts as to whether the invalid is suffering from a chill or a more serious highly contagious disease, the vet's advice should be sought immediately.

Conjunctivitis An unpleasant condition which eventually results in the eyes becoming swollen and closed. In its early stages it causes copious watering and obvious irritation, the sick bird rubbing its eyes along the perch in an effort to relieve the pain.

Aureomycin has proved valuable in treating this infectious condition. Alternatively, chloromycetin drops can prove effective if the treatment is started in the early stages.

Swollen Feet A condition sometimes seen in softbilled species and usually caused by incorrect diet or unsuitable perches, or a combination of both. The affected parts should be painted with iodine; natural perches of varying thickness should be used if it is necessary to cage the bird while treatment is carried out.

Particular attention should be paid to the bird's food. Too rich a diet with a high protein content can lead to problems of this nature.

Moulting Healthy birds usually moult without difficulty, but occasionally some cannot complete the process successfully. The moult is a particularly stamina-sapping operation and birds which have been incorrectly housed or fed may not be able to complete it in a normal way. Plenty of nourishing food will help; a humid atmosphere is also conducive to its successful completion.

Once again it is necessary to emphasise the need for correct feeding and housing in order to minimise such difficulties.

Constipation Usually easily diagnosed by the bird's inability to pass a motion; straining and a general air of discomfort. The cause is usually incorrect feeding; in the case of softbills, perhaps a lack of fibrous materials or roughage in the diet.

Two or three drops of olive oil given directly into the bill, or five drops of Syrup of Buckthorn in about an egg-cupful of water will usually effect a cure.

Egg Binding Frequently caused by cold weather when the female is in process of egg laying. The bird will usually be found huddled on the aviary floor – wings drooped and with feathers puffed out. In catching the bird it is important that she is handled with care to prevent any possibility of the egg being broken while still in the oviduct.

The bird should be placed at once in a hospital cage with the temperature set at 30 °C (85 °F). This will usually rectify the problem within a very short time. If there are further difficulties a veterinary surgeon should be consulted.

Mice While not normally included in a chapter dealing with avian diseases, it is worth pointing out the damage that can be caused should mice gain entry to the aviary or birdroom. Quite apart from upsetting nesting birds they are also carriers of a number of extremely unpleasant diseases, including salmonellosis.

Every effort should be made to prevent these and other rodents coming into contact with the birds. Once they have established a foothold they prove exceedingly difficult to eliminate.

Acclimatisation Newly obtained birds need considerable care during their first few weeks in a changed environment and climate. Many of them suffer acute stress at this time and they should be given full opportunity to recover and settle into their new home.

At first they should be housed in a spacious cage and placed in a quiet spot in the house or birdroom where they will be disturbed as little as possible. Temperature should be maintained at a reasonable level – say, around 18 to 20 °C (60 to 65 °F) for the first couple of weeks, after which it can be gradually reduced. Birds obtained during spring or summer have an enormous advantage over those acquired during the colder months of the year when they face long nights as well as low temperatures. It is an advantage to provide your birds with a period of two or three hours extra light if they are acquired during the winter. Ensure they are settled on their perches before switching off the light.

So far as diet is concerned, seedeaters, nectar feeders and fruit-eating softbills rarely present problems. Insectivorous softbills can be difficult if they are not accustomed to substitute foods. They should be provided with a variety of live foods, mixed with their insectile mixture. Most of them will eventually accept the latter if it is offered to them in this way.

Seedeaters should not be given free access to grit for the first two or three weeks. They will often eat vast quantities, with fatal results.

Breeding The ability to persuade exotic birds to breed in aviaries is perhaps the hallmark of an experienced and competent aviculturist. For many species there are still no real guide-lines to indicate proven methods of housing, feeding and other techniques which may result in a successful breeding.

Accurate notes should be made of everything that goes on in the breeding aviary, down to the smallest detail if the birds in question have been bred on only rare occasions. It is only by meticulously recording vital information that our knowledge will increase to the point where many more rare and exciting species can be bred in controlled conditions.

In general terms a quiet and secluded aviary is almost essential if birds are to be induced to nest. For with few exceptions they are nervous creatures, and they tend to become even more shy and secretive during the breeding season. Plenty of natural cover should be provided. Exotic cultivated plants are not necessary. In fact some of the most interesting breeding achievements have taken place in flights which have purposely been allowed to grow wild, with native plants providing wonderfully natural conditions.

Never be tempted to disturb a nesting pair. The flight should have a small hatch or door so that food and water can be replenished without the need to enter the aviary. If birds are seen to be constructing a nest in an exposed part of the flight every effort should be made to shield the site with rigid translucent plastic sheet. Many a brood of youngsters has been lost through torrential rain beating down on a totally unprotected nest in an aviary.

Beginner's luck only rarely produces an outstanding breeding achievement. Factors which are much more likely to influence the end result are experience, skill, patience and a real 'feeling' for one's birds. A combination which will not be acquired overnight, but one to which every aviculturist should aspire.

Yellow-backed Whydah (*Coliuspasser macrourus*)
West Africa

Description 215 mm (8½ in.) – in breeding plumage. At other times, 150 mm (6 in.). Almost entirely black – with the exception of the shoulders and mantle which are yellow; wing feathers edged with brown. Bill black; legs dark brown.

Females are usually slightly smaller. The upper surfaces are dull brown with darker striations; chin and throat with a faint yellowish tinge; underparts whitish with some darker streaks. Out-of-colour males have a similar plumage.

General Management These birds are not widely kept, possibly because they are not so spectacular in appearance as some of the long-tailed whydahs. They are easily managed, become very hardy and will live for many years in an outdoor aviary.

Although not generally aggressive, they are best not housed with smaller birds. A pair should have a roomy aviary to themselves. Provide plenty of cover in the form of shrubs, bushes and tussocks of coarse grasses. If the birds are to be housed outdoors throughout the year some kind of shelter is necessary, although these birds will frequently elect to roost in the open flight. They can stand low temperatures, but like many other exotic species they are not happy in wet or damp conditions, particularly during the winter months.

Breeding Breeding this species is a far from easy task for the aviculturist. They are not parasitic but are believed to be polygamous. It would be advisable to house three or four females with one male in the breeding aviary. Nest-building is carried out by the male whydah. Plenty of dried grass, rootlets and similar materials should be supplied. Females, once attracted to a nest, will line it with softer rootlets or even feathers. This process is continued when egg laying and incubation take place so that the original, rather flimsy, construction takes on a much more substantial appearance by the time the chicks are due to hatch.

The male, having persuaded a mate to take up residence, once mating has taken place takes no further part in the domestic routine. Incubation (about 13 days) and rearing is carried out entirely by the female. Within the relatively close confines of an aviary a careful watch must be maintained to see that the male does not chase or persecute his mate while she is incubating or rearing chicks.

The young are fed on a variety of live insects, sprouted seeds, seeding grasses, etc.

Feeding Yellow-backed Whydahs are easily fed. They should have a staple seed diet of plain canary seed, white, yellow and panicum millets, with spray millet and seeding grasses from time to time. Occasional live food is also beneficial. Individual birds seem to vary a great deal in their willingness to take green foods, but a selection should be provided. Grit and cuttlefish bone must always be available.

Weaverbirds consist of four subfamilies: typical weavers (Ploceinae), Whydahs or widow weavers (Viduinae), the sparrow weavers (Passerinae) and the buffalo weavers (Bubalornithae). By far the greatest number of weaver species come from Africa, from where the group originated, but now they have spread widely throughout the world. Perhaps the most common and widespread weaver is the familiar House Sparrow (*Passer domesticus*).

Most weavers are gregarious and are known for the intricate woven nests which some of them build. Some build a communal structure and others have a rather untidy and crude collection of grasses and sticks in which to raise their family.

Napoleon Weaver (*Euplectes afra*) West Africa

Description 130 mm (5 in.). In full nuptial plumage the male is one of the most striking-looking of all African finches. Forehead, cheeks, throat, belly and under surfaces black; remainder of the plumage bright yellow, except for the wings and tail which are brown. Bill black; legs flesh-coloured.

Females and out-of-colour males are mainly brown with darker striations and paler underparts.

General Management Hardy and easily kept, they are seen at their best in a garden aviary. Several may be kept together when the males are out of colour but in the breeding season they are best isolated into groups of up to six females with one male.

While females are peaceful little birds the same cannot be said of their busybody mates which, during the nest-building season, buzz around the aviary hissing and spluttering like runaway soda-siphons.

Although they are a colourful spectacle in full breeding plumage, it has to be admitted that both sexes present a drab and somewhat uninteresting picture at other times.

Breeding Like most weavers, the Napoleon cannot be regarded as a free breeder under controlled conditions. But a group, housed in an aviary to themselves, might produce results.

Males build a number of nests among tall-growing vegetation, such as ornamental grass or maize. Incubation and rearing is undertaken by the female, while the male sets out to attract another member of his little harem to occupy a nest. Although he plays no part in family matters he maintains a vigilant guard over his breeding territory and will defend it against any intruders.

Incubation lasts about 13 days and the young leave the nest some three weeks later. Rearing food should include plenty of live insects, sprouted seeds and green food.

Feeding A mixture of small plain canary seed, millets, including spray millet, green food and a few maggots or mealworms each day will suit these birds well. In a planted aviary they pick up a lot of natural live food – essential for their health and well-being and almost certainly having a pronounced effect on the continued brilliance of the male's nuptial plumage. If forced to exist on a seed diet alone, male Napoleon Weavers usually suffer some loss of colour. Grit and cuttlefish bone should always be available.

Half-masked Weaver (*Ploceus vitellinus*)

Tropical West Africa

Vitelline Weaver

Description 130 mm (5 in.). A popular and easily managed little weaver. Males are extremely handsome in breeding plumage. Face and cheeks black; forehead and a small area on the upper breast chestnut; top of head, nape and under surfaces golden yellow, suffused with orange on the breast; back, wings and tail olive with darker markings. Bill black; legs flesh-coloured.

Females are mainly brown, lighter on the under surfaces and with dark striations. Out-of-colour males resemble them but have slightly more distinctive and clearly defined markings on the back.

General Management Hardy and easily managed, like most other weavers this species is at its best in a large, planted aviary where the males will indulge in apparently endless bouts of nest-building during the breeding season. The Half-masked Weaver is an indefatigable builder and will frequently adorn an aviary with a dozen or more nests, neatly suspended from the branches of shrubs or bushes.

Although most often kept in pairs it is possible that this gregarious little bird would prove a more frequent and successful breeder if several were housed in a really spacious aviary.

Breeding The male is a busy and extremely energetic little bird during the breeding season, dividing his time between building nests and trying to persuade any females in the vicinity to inspect his handiwork as a prelude to mating and laying eggs.

Plenty of nest-building material should be supplied. Raffia is useful but the birds will make use of practically any kind of grass-like material, preferably including some with fairly broad leaves.

The Half-masked Weaver has been bred on several occasions in aviaries. Incubation of the three or four eggs is carried out by the female; the eggs take 12 days to hatch.

Plenty of live food together with sprouted seeds and various seeding grasses should be supplied when young are being reared. Ant pupae, smooth caterpillars, flies and similar items should supplement the small mealworms and maggots which these birds will take to feed their chicks.

Feeding A staple diet of mixed millets with some plain canary seed suits them well. They should also have millet sprays and bunches of seeding grasses. Chickweed, groundsel and other greenstuff should be offered regularly. They will benefit greatly from a small ration of mealworms or maggots each day – no more than two or three per bird is necessary. They must always have access to grit and cuttlefish bone.

Pin-tailed Whydah (*Vidua macroura*)
Africa south of the Sahara

Description 300 mm (12 in.) – including the male's long tail feathers in nuptial plumage. At other times 130 mm (5 in.). Head, nape, back, wings and tail glossy black; the remainder of the plumage white. Bill coral-red; legs slate-coloured.

Females are mainly brown with darker streaks on the upper surfaces; throat whitish; breast and underparts buff. Out of colour, the male has a similar plumage.

General Management This popular and widely-kept little whydah is regarded as something of a villain in avicultural circles. In breeding condition the males are extremely aggressive and should be housed in spacious quarters if trouble is to be avoided.

They are easy to acclimatise and can be wintered in an outdoor aviary. In-colour males are an attractive sight with their rather buoyant flight – tail feathers streaming out behind them as they indulge in their courtship display. They have a rather falcon-like habit of diving to ground level, either from a high perch or while hovering around the females they are hoping to attract. Quite often this headlong dash ends at the seed dish and effectively disperses any other birds in the vicinity.

Breeding The Pin-tailed Whydah is polygamous and parasitic. The host species vary, depending to a great extent on the geographic location of the birds. St Helena, Red-eared and Orange-cheeked Waxbills are known to be parasitised by this whydah.

A successful formula for breeding would therefore have to include a small breeding colony of one of the host species as well as a male and up to half a dozen female Pin-tailed Whydahs. In a controlled environment it is far from easy to synchronise the breeding cycle of two species; most aviculturists are only too well aware of the difficulty of persuading the host species to nest successfully – without the additional complication of bringing whydahs to the peak of their activity at about the same time. It is, however, a challenging prospect and one which is well worth attempting.

If whydah eggs are laid in the nest of one of the host waxbills, the foster-parents should be provided with plenty of sprouted seeds, seeding grass heads and small live food – aphis, blackfly, ant pupae and the like. The young whydahs will be raised alongside the rightful occupants of the nest.

Feeding Like most whydahs, this species enjoys some live food at all times. Plain canary seed, yellow, panicum and spray millets provide the basic diet. Three or four mealworms or maggots can be given each day. Some green food should also be supplied together with grit and cuttlefish bone.

Pin-tailed Whydahs have an amusing habit of scratching vigorously – using both feet rather after the manner of a domestic fowl – in loose earth or even the feeding dish. It is a mannerism shared by related species.

Fischer's Whydah (*Vidua fischeri*) East Africa

Description 300 mm (12 in.) – including the male's elegant tail feathers during the breeding season. At other times 125 mm (5 in.). One of the most beautiful members of a genus well known for the remarkable development of the males' plumage during the breeding season. In full colour the male Fischer's Whydah is a handsome combination of mainly blue-black, buff and cream. Bill and legs red.

Females and out-of-colour males are inconspicuous, sparrow-like little birds; mainly brown with darker striations; under surfaces pale grey-brown. Bill and legs pinkish brown.

General Management Although the Viduine whydahs are hardy and easy to manage in aviaries they present a number of problems for the aviculturist intent on achieving breeding results. They are both polygamous and parasitic; it is exceedingly difficult, under normal control conditions, to persuade these spectacular birds to produce eggs in the nests of appropriate host species.

Fischer's Whydahs are found in the more arid and dry parts of East Africa and Somalia. When acclimatised they can withstand low temperatures – but damp conditions may prove harmful.

They can be wintered in an outdoor aviary provided they have a comfortable and frost-free shelter.

Breeding Ideally, a male Fischer's Whydah should be housed with a harem of three or four females. In breeding condition the male is very much master in his own household and although one would not describe his behaviour as murderous he is likely to chase and bully smaller companions.

A further complication with this parasitic species is that eggs appear to be laid in the nest of only one specific host – the Purple Grenadier Waxbill (*Granatina ianthinogaster*). So that before there can be any hopes of successfully breeding the whydahs there must already be a nesting pair of grenadiers in the same aviary. This is a daunting task – for these colourful waxbills are themselves delicate and difficult to breed in confinement. If one is fortunate enough to achieve a double breeding success with the two species, the young of both will be reared – by the waxbills – only if a regular supply of small live food is provided.

Live ant pupae, wasp grubs, greenfly, blackfly, fruit flies (a wingless mutation would be most suitable in an outdoor aviary), spiders and small smooth caterpillars would be essential. Sprouted seeds together with seeding grass heads and green food must also be supplied.

Feeding A staple diet of small millets and plain canary seed provides a good basic diet for Fischer's Whydahs. They should also have spray millet and some sprouted seeds. They enjoy mealworms and small maggots.

Grit and cuttlefish bone must always be available.

Cut-throat Finch (*Amadina fasciata*) Tropical Africa
Ribbon Finch

Description 130 mm (5 in.). Mainly beige-brown in colour with darker markings producing an attractive scale-like appearance. The male has a broad band of scarlet across the throat. Bill lead-coloured; legs pinkish brown.

Females are similar but lack the red throat marking.

General Management Popular and easily managed, they are easy to house and feed, hardy and not difficult to breed if conditions are right. In most respects they are excellent birds for the beginner.

When first obtained they should be housed in a roomy cage or indoor flight until they have adjusted to any change of climate. Aviary-bred birds are occasionally obtainable but it can be assumed that those available from dealers are wild-taken specimens, and as such they should be treated carefully until acclimatised.

Cut-throats are tough little birds which can eventually be housed outside throughout the year. They should be provided with a comfortable shelter for use during the winter, but heat is not necessary.

Stoutly built and with a heavy, conical bill, they are well able to take care of themselves in mixed company. Individual birds vary a good deal in temperament; some are content merely to assert themselves at the feeding dish; others become really aggressive and make life very difficult for smaller or weaker companions.

Breeding There seems no reason why, if aviculturists will make the effort, these little birds should not breed with the same freedom as Zebra Finches and Bengalese. Cut-throats should be good subjects for the sort of 'domestication' which is essential if they are to have a secure avicultural future.

They make use of nest-boxes or baskets, building an untidy nest of dry grasses, hay, rootlets, etc. Feathers are often used to line the finished structure before the clutch of up to six eggs is laid. Incubation is undertaken by both sexes. The eggs hatch after 12 days.

The chicks are not difficult to rear if their parents are provided with appropriate food supplements. In addition to their normal seed diet they should have some soaked seeds, small live food, sponge cake soaked in honey, and some insectile mixture.

Feeding Plain canary seed, various millets, green food and whatever seeding grasses can be gathered from the fields and hedgerows will provide all that Cut-throats need to remain in good health. Essential additions are grit and cuttlefish bone. Some aviculturists mix cod-liver oil with the birds' staple seed diet. This is beneficial, particularly during the winter months, and may also help to combat egg-binding in the females – a problem which arises fairly frequently with this species.

Finches The most characteristic feature of the finches is the bill which has normally a short conical shape adapted for eating seeds. For this reason they are sometimes called hardbills. Although their primary requirement is seed, many require fruit and insects in their diet, especially at times of breeding.

Java Sparrow (*Padda oryzivora*) Indonesia
Java Rice Bird

Description 140 mm (5½ in.). One of the most popular and instantly recognised foreign finches. Also available in white and pied forms. Head and tail black; cheeks white; remainder of plumage soft grey; ring of bare skin around eye red. Bill pink; legs flesh-coloured. The sexes are alike.

General Management Acclimatised Java Sparrows can be kept in an outdoor aviary throughout the year. With care they will live for many years. Although not particularly aggressive they are best not housed with smaller species; their formidable bill provides a clear indication that they can look after themselves in mixed company.

Breeding While the white and pied forms are free breeders in captivity, the wild grey Java Sparrow has nested only infrequently.

They should be provided with an open-fronted nest-box and plenty of dry grass and rootlets with which to build their rather bulky nest.

The young are not difficult to rear and the only addition necessary to the adults' normal diet at this time is some sprouted seed.

Feeding A mixture of plain canary seed and millet suits these birds admirably. They are also fond of hemp (given sparingly) and paddy rice. Greenstuff should be offered. Grit and cuttlefish bone must always be available.

Spicebird (*Lonchura punctulata*)
India and Ceylon eastwards to China
Nutmeg Finch, Spotted Munia

Description 115 mm (4½ in.). Very popular and widely kept little mannikins. Easy to keep and becomes very hardy. Upper surfaces and head chocolate-brown; underparts white, each feather edged with dark brown to produce a scale-like effect. Bill black; legs dark grey. The sexes are alike.

General Management An excellent species for the beginner. They can be housed in outdoor aviaries throughout the year. They do not need heated quarters but should be provided with a dry shelter and perhaps nest-boxes for use as dormitories.

Breeding Although breeding successes have been recorded with this species they cannot be described as free breeders. They make use of both boxes and baskets but need a secluded site and should be disturbed as little as possible once nesting is under way.

Between four and eight eggs are laid; they hatch after about 13 days. The youngsters are usually reared without problems if their parents are provided with plenty of sprouted seeds, millet sprays, green food and some insects.

Feeding Spicebirds are simplicity itself to feed. They thrive on a mixture of plain canary seed and millet; also millet sprays and green food. Grit and cuttlefish bone should always be available.

African Silverbill (*Euodice malabarica cantans*)

West and Central Africa

Warbling Silverbill

Description 100 mm (4 in.). Neat and attractive little birds. They are an excellent choice for the novice aviculturist. Head and upper surfaces creamy brown; wings darker brown; underparts pale buff; rump and tail black. Bill silvery grey; legs brown.

The sexes are alike.

General Management These adaptable little birds thrive in most types of accommodation. When acclimatised they can remain in an outdoor aviary throughout the year but must be provided with dry and frost-free sleeping accommodation.

Since they are common and lack distinctive markings, few aviculturists are willing to devote separate aviary accommodation to these birds. Like most other species, breeding success is more likely if they can be provided with a small aviary to themselves – but they will often go to nest in a mixed community of other small seedeaters. They are completely inoffensive and care must be taken to see that they are not housed with more pugnacious species which would upset any chances of successful breeding.

Silverbills are difficult birds to sex. The only sure guide is the male's song and it is sensible to obtain several birds from which to select true pairs.

Breeding True pairs of silverbills usually prove to be extremely prolific. They will make use of boxes or baskets in which to construct their nest. Some pairs share the Zebra Finch's bad habit of building another nest base on top of a clutch of eggs. If this problem arises it can sometimes be overcome by filling up the nest-box or basket with tightly packed material so that the birds have only a small amount of space in which to build and lay.

The usual clutch consists of four eggs which hatch after 13 days. The young are easily reared and the parents require little other than seed, sprouted seeds and greenstuff for rearing purposes.

Two or three broods are usually produced. Some aviculturists have used these birds to hatch and rear the young of more difficult species in much the same manner in which Bengalese are employed as foster-parents.

There seems no reason why silverbills should not be domesticated to the same degree as Zebra Finches. The fact that they have been inexpensive and are among the most freely available of small seedeaters has almost certainly been the main reason why efforts have not been made to produce genuine aviary-bred strains.

Feeding Silverbills require little other than plain canary seed and mixed millets. Spray millet can be given as an occasional treat and green food should be regularly available. They must also have grit and cuttlefish bone.

Bengalese – Domesticated
Society Finch

Description 130 mm (5 in.). Strictly speaking, not a pure species, but a fertile hybrid, produced by the Japanese, and appearing to have been bred from various members of the genus *Lonchura*. An ideal bird for the beginner and available in many forms, including white, shades of brown and white and also crested varieties. All are rather heavy-bodied little birds with a typical Munia-like bill.

The sexes are almost indistinguishable, apart from the male's little warbling song.

General Management They are easy to manage, thriving in almost any accommodation from a small canary-breeding cage to a garden aviary. Unless disturbed by the other species, they should be successful in breeding in with a mixed group of birds. They will winter successfully without heat, either roosting in a shelter or in nest-boxes.

They have well-developed maternal instincts and are frequently used as foster-parents for other finches which have an uncertain temperament during the breeding season. This instinct is so strongly developed that a pair of Bengalese will often try to take over the nest of completely unrelated species in a community aviary.

Breeding They will use a box in which to build a rather untidy nest. From four to eight eggs are usually laid. It is difficult to say which parent undertakes the incubation since both male and female will frequently be found sitting side by side on the nest. The eggs hatch after 14 days and both parents share the task of rearing the young. The chicks can be reared without addition to their parents' normal seed diet.

Feeding Plain canary seed, and millet. Millet sprays and sprouted seeds can be regarded more as a luxury than as essential. Grit and cuttlefish bone should always be available.

Black-headed Mannikin (*Lonchura malacca atricapilla*)
India
Black-headed Munia, Black-headed Nun

Description 115 mm (4½ in.). An easily managed little seedeater. Head, neck and throat glossy black; remainder of the plumage dark chestnut, except for a patch of black on the abdomen. Bill silvery grey; legs dark grey. The sexes are alike.

General Management These attractive little birds are very easy to keep. They quickly become hardy and thrive in a garden aviary. In confinement their claws have a tendency to grow very long. When this occurs they should be trimmed to prevent them catching in vegetation or wire-netting.

Breeding Although one of the most commonly kept seedeaters, breeding successes with the Black-headed Mannikin have been few. Sexing difficulties may be a contributory factor, plus the fact that they have been so easily acquired few aviculturists have really tried to persuade them to go to nest. They build a bulky, domed nest and might use an oval nesting-basket. Alternatively, a handful of twigs and coarse grasses fixed securely in place among vegetation could tempt them.

Plenty of seeding grasses, sprouted seeds, including millet sprays, and small live food should be provided if chicks are to be reared.

Feeding Black-headed Mannikins thrive on a mixture of millets and plain canary seed. Spray millet and seeding grass heads provide welcome variety. They should also have regular supplies of green food. Grit and cuttlefish bone must always be available.

Cherry Finch (*Aidemosyne modesta*) Eastern Australia
Plum-head Finch

Description 115 mm (4½ in.). An attractive little bird – although much less brightly coloured than most Australian seedeaters. Upper surfaces dull tawny brown with some white spots on the wings; crown and throat plum-coloured; underparts off-white barred with brown. Bill black; legs brown.

Females are similar but lack the throat patch.

General Management This pleasant little bird has never been a very popular aviary subject. Birds from Australia used to have a habit of dying, although appearing to be in good health. Post-mortem examination invariably revealed congestion of the lungs or pneumonia. This problem should no longer arise since the only stock available is aviary-bred.

Although individual birds appear hardy enough to winter in outdoor aviaries it is not advisable to risk the species under very cold conditions. They are probably better housed indoors for the duration of the winter.

Breeding An established pair of Cherry Finches, given a small aviary to themselves, will usually go to nest, but with varying degrees of success.

They will nest in a globular wicker basket. Incubation of the four to six eggs lasts 12 days and is shared by both parents.

There is nothing more disappointing for the aviculturist than to have a pair of birds success-fully hatch a brood of chicks, only to abandon them soon afterwards. Cherry Finches can be excellent parents if conditions are right; but if they are subjected to any interference, either from their owner or other aviary occupants, they are likely to desert their brood very quickly. The adults' diet should be supplemented with sprouted seeds, some insectile mixture (mixed in small quantities with the seed), extra green food and live insects. Small mealworms can be given but live ant pupae are much more valuable if available.

Feeding Cherry Finches are easy to feed. They should have a staple diet of plain canary seed, yellow and panicum millets, millet sprays and plenty of green food. Live insects are not essential but they enjoy an occasional mealworm. Alternatively any small live food which can be collected in the garden should be offered. They should have seeding and sprouting grasses as often as possible. Grit and cuttlefish bone are essential.

It is possible that a varied diet is a solution to some of the problems which aviculturists have encountered with this species. It would be unwise to overload their diet with foods which are very rich and have a high protein content.

Gouldian Finch (*Poephila gouldiae*) Northern Australia

Lady Gould Finch

Description 130 mm (5 in.). One of the most colourful of all finches. Lower neck, mantle and wings grass-green; chest bright purple; lower breast and abdomen saffron-yellow; back of the head and rump lilac; face and head red bordered with black. Bill horn-coloured; legs flesh-coloured.

Females are similar but the colours are less bright.

Black-headed and Yellow-headed forms are also available.

General Management Gouldian Finches can be housed outdoors throughout the summer months and are peaceful with other species. Their breeding season coincides with a European autumn so it is essential they are housed indoors when nesting takes place. Roomy flights in a slightly heated birdroom provide the most suitable type of breeding quarters.

Given a balanced diet and suitable accommodation, there is no reason why aviculturists should not enjoy consistent success with these beautiful little finches.

Although Gouldians are bred and exported in considerable numbers by the Japanese, European-bred stock is much easier to establish.

Breeding Nest-boxes or globular wicker baskets should be provided – together with plenty of suitable nesting material.

Gouldian Finches can be very prolific and a good breeding pair is capable of producing three nests of up to six eggs each during the course of a season.

The youngsters are easily reared. Sprouted seed should be provided. Seeding grasses and extra green food are also valuable rearing foods.

Some fanciers prefer to entrust incubation and rearing to Bengalese foster-parents, transferring the eggs as soon as the clutch is complete.

Feeding There are many theories about correct diet for these birds. Various vitamin supplements are recommended together with such items as granulated charcoal, mineralised grits, etc. There is little doubt that correct diet is an important factor in achieving success with Gouldian Finches. Those who are intent on specialising in these and other grassfinches are recommended to join one of the societies catering for this branch of the hobby; expert guidance based on the experience of other aviculturists is readily available.

Millets contribute substantially to the staple diet. Yellow, panicum and spray millets should be offered regularly together with some small plain canary seed. Green food should always be available together with grit and cuttlefish bone.

Star Finch (*Bathilda ruficauda*) Northern Australia
Ruficauda, Rufous-tailed Finch

Description 130 mm (5 in.). A popular and easily bred Australian grassfinch. Upper surfaces olive-green; breast olive; lower underparts paler yellowish green; forehead, cheeks and throat bright red; tail rufous; face and breast spotted white. Bill red; legs flesh-coloured. Females are similar but usually show less red around the face.

General Management Star Finches are easily managed birds. They can be bred in cages, but are probably more successful in small compartment aviaries. They are reasonably hardy but should not be exposed to extremes of cold or wet weather during the winter months.

Breeding An established pair, housed in a suitable small flight, will often produce three broods in the course of a season. They will use a box or wicker basket for nesting purposes.
The three or four eggs hatch after about 14 days and the young are usually reared without difficulty. Plenty of millet sprays, seeding grasses, green food and some small live food should be provided at this time.

Feeding A basic diet for Star Finches consists of small plain canary seed, white, yellow and panicum millets. They are fond of green food and seeding grass heads. They must always have access to grit and cuttlefish bone.

Zebra Finch (*Taeniopygia castanotis*) Australia

Description 115 mm (4½ in.). Almost too well known to need a description, the Zebra Finch is now available in a wide range of colours and is regarded as domesticated. Mainly grey in colour with buff or white underparts; bright chestnut ear patch and flanks, the latter spotted with white; throat barred black and white; white patch between bill and eye. Bill red; legs orange.

General Management Probably the ideal species with which to start a collection of aviary birds. Very easy to house, feed and breed. They should have a comfortable shelter for use during periods of severe weather, but take care to remove all nest-boxes during the winter months. Apart from using them for roosting, there is every possibility that Zebras will continue breeding right through the year if given opportunity.

Breeding Zebras will use either nest-baskets or boxes. Provide plenty of nesting material and also ensure that there is a solid wad of hay or dried grass already in their nesting container. They have a bad habit of building a nest in an empty box, laying a clutch of eggs – and repeating the process again and again until all the space is taken up with alternative layers of nests and eggs.

The chicks are reared without addition to the birds' normal diet – although sprouted seed is, as always, a useful addition.

Feeding A staple diet of plain canary seed, yellow and panicum millets will keep Zebra Finches in excellent health. An occasional millet spray is a great treat. Supply them with plenty of green food – chickweed, groundsel, etc. Grit and cuttlefish bone should always be available.

Heck's Grassfinch (*Poephila acuticauda hecki*)

North-western Australia

Description 165 mm (6½ in.). A beautifully neat and well-groomed little bird which lives and breeds well in aviaries. This red-billed race is probably less widely kept than the typical yellow-billed Long-tailed Grassfinch (*P. acuticauda*). Head silvery grey; upper surfaces and wings pale fawn-grey, a darker shade on the wings; underparts fawn; large oval throat patch black; eye stripe black; thigh markings black edged with white; tail black. Bill red; legs orange.

The sexes are almost alike, but females will usually be found to have slightly smaller bib patches than the males.

General Management Aviary-bred stock is frequently available and a good breeding pair is a worthwhile acquisition. They are not easy to sex and great care should be exercised in selecting two birds, unless they are a guaranteed pair.

They are reasonably hardy birds. An outdoor aviary suits them well during the summer months but unless it has heated shelter the birds are best housed in roomy flights in a birdroom during the colder months. Some aviculturists keep them successfully in unheated accommodation throughout the year but the author prefers to house them in a frost-free atmosphere during winter. Much depends, of course, on the severity of the weather; it has been possible to keep species much more delicate than the Heck's Grassfinch in unheated aviaries during mild winters.

A pair should be given a small aviary to themselves as they are quite aggressive when breeding, and in any case are much more likely to nest successfully if housed alone.

Breeding Heck's Grassfinches will usually build their nest in a nest-basket or box. One or two alternative sites should be provided in their aviary.

Usually four or five eggs are laid. Incubation, which takes up to 17 days, is shared by both male and female. No special foods are required for rearing, although sprouted seeds and extra millet sprays will be appreciated. Some aviculturists provide live food – a few mealworms per day – but others have found few birds of this species which seemed interested, either in or out of the breeding season.

Many pairs will raise three broods in the course of a season. Take care to see that nest-boxes are removed once that point has been reached, otherwise the birds are likely to attempt breeding throughout the year.

Feeding Heck's Grassfinches will thrive on a simple diet of plain canary seed and mixed millets. Millet sprays and seeding grasses provide valuable additions and green food should also be offered regularly, although here again individual birds vary a great deal in their willingness to take it. They should always have access to grit and cuttlefish bone.

Pin-tailed Nonpareil (*Erythrura prasina*)

Burma, Malaysia, Sumatra, Borneo and Java

Pin-tailed Parrot Finch

Description 140 mm (5½ in.). The most easily obtained member of a genus which includes some of the most highly prized birds in aviculture. Males are mainly grass-green with a blue face and throat; lower breast, rump and tail bright red. The central feathers of the tail are extended into points. Bill black; legs flesh-coloured.

Females are similar but lack the blue face and red under surfaces. They also have a shorter tail.

General Management Although easily obtainable, this is not really a bird for the beginner. Newly acquired Pin-tailed Nonpareils can prove difficult during acclimatisation and are best kept only by experienced aviculturists.

They are inclined to be somewhat wild and nervous. They frequently indulge in headlong flight, coming into collision with the first object to impede their path. Since, in the average aviary or birdroom, this is most likely to be either wire-netting or glass, the birds can suffer severely from such activity.

Once acclimatised and settled into a planted aviary they prove very hardy and can be wintered without heat. Housed in cages or very small aviaries they tend to become over-fat. They are gross feeders and somewhat disinclined to take exercise. A spacious, planted flight usually helps overcome this problem.

Breeding This is one of those species in which males invariably seem to outnumber females. Probably 90 per cent of 'true pairs' purchased from dealers eventually turn out to be two males. An immense number of immature birds are sold as females, quite inadvertently. The genuine article – moulted-out females of the species – can be rather difficult to locate.

Like most of their relatives, a fit and compatible pair of Pin-tailed Nonpareils can prove extremely prolific. They are best given a small aviary to themselves and provided with baskets or boxes in which to build their nest. Occasionally they will build in a bush or against a creeper-clad wall. Incubation is shared by both sexes and the eggs hatch after 13 days.

Rearing is usually accomplished without difficulty. The parents should be supplied with sprouted seeds and some small live food to supplement their staple diet at this time.

Feeding Newly obtained Pin-tails are sometimes difficult to accustom to a seed diet. It is a good plan to mix gradually increasing quantities of plain canary seed with paddy rice during the first few weeks after acquisition. Most birds will soon start to pick over other seeds, and eventually paddy rice can be eliminated from the diet. Slow starters should be housed with other seedeaters for a while; they will learn by example to accept a more varied diet.

Eventually they can be offered a mixed seed diet including plain canary, white and yellow millets. They should also have green food and germinated seeds. Grit and cuttlefish bone should always be available.

Diamond Sparrow (*Steganopleura guttata*) Australia

Description 115 mm (4½ in.). A strikingly-marked Australian finch which breeds freely in aviaries, if a true pair can be obtained. Head, upper surfaces and wings grey; rump crimson; under surfaces white, with a broad black band across the upper breast; flanks and tail black, the former liberally spotted with white; black stripe through eye. Bill red; legs lead-coloured. The sexes are alike.

General Management Since the export of these birds from Australia is banned one can assume that new stock has been aviary-bred and the question of acclimatisation should not arise.
They are excellent occupants of a garden aviary and hardy enough to remain outdoors without heat throughout the winter months. A comfortable shelter should be available.

Breeding Diamond Sparrows will make use of a box or basket, or even build their own nest in a bush. It is a fairly bulky structure made of grass and other fibrous materials.
Four to six eggs are laid and incubation is shared by both sexes; the eggs hatch after 14 days. In addition to their normal seed diet, the parents should be supplied with plenty of sprouted seeds, additional greenstuff and some live food while they are feeding their young.

Feeding These birds need little other than canary seed and millet outside the breeding season. This basic menu can be varied with green food, seeding grasses and sprouted seeds. Grit and cuttlefish bone are essential at all times.

Green Avadavat (*Amandava formosa*) Central India

Description 100 mm (4 in.). One of the few predominantly green and yellow waxbills. Upper surfaces bright grass-green; chin and throat yellowish grey; breast and underparts bright yellow; flanks white heavily barred with black; tail black. Bill red; legs flesh-coloured.

Although the female's markings are similar they are less clearly defined and the colours are much more dull.

General Management Rather delicate when first imported and not recommended for beginners. Very much inclined to feather-pluck if closely confined for any length of time.

When acclimatised they are reasonably hardy but are probably happier given slight heat during the colder months. They settle down well in a small, planted garden aviary – essential accommodation if they are to remain fit and in good plumage. They are never at their best in damp conditions.

Breeding Not a very free breeder in controlled conditions. The Green Avadavat may accept a wicker nest-basket but a pair intent on breeding are more likely to build their own nest in a low bush or similar vegetation.

A varied and plentiful supply of small insects will be required if the young are to be successfully reared.

Feeding A staple diet consists of a millet mixture – yellow and panicum with some plain canary seed. Spray millet should be offered regularly together with sprouted seeds. They are fond of live food and should be given a daily ration of any insects that are obtainable. They must always have a supply of grit and cuttlefish bone.

Red Avadavat (*Amandava amandava*)

India and Ceylon eastwards to Burma and Malaysia

Tiger Finch, Bombay Avadavat, Red Munia

Description 100 mm (4 in.). The only waxbill to have an eclipse plumage – when males moult to resemble their more soberly coloured mates. In colour, males are mainly bright red; wings dark brown, tail black; sides and breast spotted with white. Bill red; legs brown.

Females and out-of-colour males, have brown upper surfaces; chin and throat whitish; breast and underparts buff-brown; upper tail coverts red.

General Management These little waxbills have much to recommend them and are an excellent choice for the beginner. In addition to their attractive colouring, the males have a short but pleasant song; they soon become hardy and are not difficult to breed.

When acclimatised, Red Avadavats prove to be extremely hardy and are quite capable of wintering in unheated quarters. Although they can be kept in cages or indoor flights their plumage seems to deteriorate under such conditions, and with successive moults the red areas become increasingly darker – eventually even to black in extreme cases. They are far better housed in a planted aviary where they usually remain in good health and plumage for many years.

These little birds are excellent in a community of small waxbills. They are not at all aggressive and provided the aviary is not overcrowded, and that there are no birds present which will attack them, Red Avadavats are quite likely to breed in a mixed collection.

Breeding Red Avadavats provide yet another example of a species which, although not difficult to breed in aviaries, has never been fully tried by aviculturists because replacement stock has been so easily acquired.

They will make use of wicker baskets or build a nest in shrubby vegetation. They seem less partial to enclosed boxes than many small finches.

From four to six eggs are laid and incubation lasts about 12 days. When the chicks are hatched, their parents must be supplied with plenty of small live food, sprouted seeds and seeding grasses. The need for additional foods – and especially small insects – is of paramount importance for all breeding pairs of waxbills. The fact that, outside the breeding season, they can be kept on a mainly seed diet is no guide to their requirements when they have youngsters in the nest.

Feeding In addition to a mixture of yellow and panicum millets, Red Avadavats are very fond of spray millet. They can also have some small plain canary seed. Green food and seeding grasses should also be supplied. Grit and cuttlefish bone are essential.

Orange-cheeked Waxbill (*Estrilda melpoda*) West Africa

Description 100 mm (4 in.). An extremely pretty waxbill, well worthy of more attention as a breeding prospect. Crown and nape grey; upper surfaces fawn-brown; chin and throat pale grey, darker on the lower breast; rump crimson; tail black; large cheek patches bright orange. Bill red; legs horn-coloured.

The sexes are alike, although females may have a slightly smaller area of orange on the cheeks.

General Management Delightful birds in a planted aviary, but are usually rather shy and secretive. They are very active and rather 'tit-like' in their movements with an engaging habit of wagging their tails from side to side when excited or alarmed.

They become hardy when acclimatised.

Breeding There have been far too few breeding successes recorded with these charming little birds. Certainly they are inclined to somewhat abortive attempts at nesting. But the fact that they are so freely available has probably caused aviculturists to concentrate on other species. Orange-cheeked Waxbills will build in boxes or baskets, occasionally constructing a domed nest in a bush. They should not be disturbed once they show signs of wanting to nest. Four eggs is the usual clutch and these hatch after 11 days. As with most other waxbills, small live food is essential at this time. Greenfly and blackfly can often be gathered in quantity; fruit flies, smooth caterpillars and ant pupae are also valuable.

Feeding Mixed millets and canary seed, spray millet, seeding grasses and a variety of green food will keep these little birds in excellent health. They also enjoy sprouted seeds. Grit and cuttlefish bone are essential.

Waxbills A group of 107 species of Old World seedeaters of which many have been favoured by aviculturists. Their bright colours, lively nature and relatively simple adaption to confinement make them ideal aviary subjects.

The group consists of several different families including avadavats, cut-throats, cordon bleus, grenadiers, firefinches, parrotfinches, mannikins, munias and many others. All are small birds, 1500 mm (6 in.) or less, with short and pointed bills. They are mainly from tropical countries including Africa, southern Asia, Australia and the East Indies, but some species such as the St Helena Waxbill (**Estrilda astrild**) and Orange-cheeked Waxbill (**E. melpoda**) have colonised suitable habitats in other countries when taken there by man.

Their normal habitat varies from sedge and reed marshes, forest clearings and scrublands to open grassland. In the wild their seed diet is supplemented with insects and soft berries. Like the weaver birds, they are very gregarious, building their large nests in colonies. At other times they move about in very large flocks containing several species.

Golden-breasted Waxbill (*Estrilda subflava*)
Africa south of the Sahara
Zebra Waxbill

Description 90 mm (3½ in.). A neat little waxbill which, despite its size, is surprisingly hardy and lives well in aviaries. Upper surfaces dark olive; breast and abdomen yellow with flecks of bright orange; flanks yellow finely barred with grey; red eyebrow stripe. Bill red; legs flesh-coloured.

Females are similar but lack the eye stripe and have paler underparts.

General Management Golden-breasted Waxbills settle down quickly in aviaries and are not difficult to acclimatise. Although they can be left in the aviary throughout the year, it is desirable that slight heat should be provided in their shelter in cold weather.

Given a small outdoor aviary to themselves, there is every prospect of these little birds breeding. Provide some natural cover – either growing plants and shrubs or, if the flight is very small, bunches of evergreens wired into place to provide nesting sites.

Breeding Provide globular wicker baskets, open-fronted boxes or, if any can be located, one or two old weavers' nests.

Both sexes share incubation and the eggs hatch after about 12 days. Provide plenty of small live food and some sprouted seeds for rearing; the parents may also make use of some fine-grade insectile food.

Feeding Mainly millets and plain canary seed. They are very fond of millet sprays and also enjoy seeding grass heads. Provide plenty of green food. An occasional mealworm or a few maggots can be offered from time to time. Grit and cuttlefish bone must always be available.

Cordon Bleu (*Uraeginthus bengalus*) Tropical Africa
Red-cheeked Cordon Blue

Description 115 mm (4½ in.). One of the best-known and most popular of all foreign seed-eaters. Upper surfaces greyish fawn; face, cheeks and most of the under surfaces sky-blue; bright red cheek patch; lower breast and abdomen grey-brown. Bill silvery pink; legs horn-coloured.

The female has rather less blue on the underparts and lacks the red cheek patches.

General Management When acclimatised Cordon Bleus are hardy little birds which will live for many years in an aviary. They are particularly susceptible to low temperatures and damp but eventually they become tough and resilient.

Breeding Cordon Bleus can prove to be free breeders in aviaries. They usually build their own nest in a bush or similar cover; alternatively they will use an open-fronted box or nest-basket. The clutch consists of up to five eggs and both sexes take turns to incubate them for 14 days.

Small live food is essential for rearing the young. Provide some insectile mixture and a variety of greenstuff and seeding grasses. Some pairs will take sponge cake soaked in honey water.

Feeding Mixed millets and some plain canary seed provide a good basic diet for these little birds. They should also have seeding grasses and millet sprays together with various items of green food. Even outside the breeding season they should have regular supplies of insects. Grit and cuttlefish bone should always be available.

Green Twinspot (*Mandingoa nitidula*) East Africa
Green-backed Twinspot

Description 100 mm (4 in.). Not easy to establish and best kept only by experienced aviculturists. Upper surfaces and breast olive-green; flanks and lower underparts black with distinctive white spots; facial mask orange-red. Bill black; legs flesh-coloured.
Females are similar but the face mask is golden buff in colour.

General Management Green Twinspots are attractive little birds. Neat and alert, they are much sought after by many aviculturists. Unfortunately they are also among the most delicate of small seedeaters and require careful management if they are to survive. Even when acclimatised they should never be regarded as hardy, or easy to keep.

They can be housed with other small waxbills or – if breeding is hoped for – in a small compartment aviary by themselves. They can remain outside throughout the summer but must be brought indoors before the advent of colder weather. Winter accommodation should be spacious. Flights or cages should be furnished with plenty of twiggy branches to occupy the birds' interest. Housed in small cages there is every possibility that these little birds, like many related species, will indulge in feather-plucking to relieve their boredom.

Their summer aviary should be in a sheltered position. Part of the top and sides can be covered with clear polythene to provide some protection from cold winds and driving rain.

Breeding A secluded garden aviary provides the best accommodation for a breeding pair of twinspots. Success is much more likely if they are the sole occupants. Globular wicker baskets should be provided as possible nest sites.

Twinspots are highly insectivorous at all times; breeding birds will take little other than small live food when they have chicks to rear. Live ant pupae are invaluable. Unfortunately they are not easy to find and other substitute foods must be tried. The larvae of the house fly can often be purchased from angling specialists. These tiny larvae are much smaller and softer than those of the blowfly. Small flies can be attracted to the breeding aviary with a piece of rotting meat or fish. A shovelful of manure will have the same effect.

Feeding A staple diet of mixed millets and millet sprays suits these little birds. Live food is essential. Small mealworms and maggots can be given in moderation. They are also very fond of blowfly chrysalis. Spiders, smooth caterpillars and other insects should be given as often as possible. Grit and cuttlefish bone should always be available.

Melba Finch (*Pytilia melba*) Central and Southern Africa
Crimson-faced Waxbill, Green-winged Pytilia

Description 130 mm (5 in.). Pretty little African seedeaters not often obtainable. Head and throat crimson; cheeks, neck and upper back grey; lower back and wings olive-green; upper breast orange, merging into green on the under surfaces and abdomen; rump red; tail black and red; lower breast spotted white. Bill red; legs brown.
Females are paler in colour and lack the red markings on face and throat.

General Management When first obtained they should be treated with care and not put into an outside flight until they have had several weeks to settle down. If acquired in winter they should remain in heated quarters until the warmer weather arrives.
They live well in a garden aviary and a breeding pair should have a small flight to themselves. Although good mixers at most times the males become very pugnacious during the breeding season.
Whilst many aviculturists have wintered acclimatised specimens outside without heat, it is not recommended. Far better, with this and similar species, to provide spacious flights in a heated indoor birdroom during the cold weather.

Breeding Breeding results with this species have been somewhat inconsistent. Pairs will frequently go to nest, lay eggs and commence incubation – only to abandon the project without any apparent reason.
Privacy for the breeding pair is important and there should be no intrusion from anyone once nesting is seen to be under way. Choose as secluded a site as possible for the breeding aviary and see that it has plenty of cover.
Melba Finches may use an open-fronted box or basket, or construct their own domed nest in a bush. Built of dry grass, hay and rootlets, it is usually lined with feathers and these should be included with other available nesting material for the birds.
Usually four eggs are laid and the 14-day incubation period is shared by both parents. An abundant supply of small insects is vital if the chicks are to be reared successfully.

Feeding Even outside the breeding season Melba Finches are quite insectivorous and will not live long if offered a straightforward seed diet. They should have a standard finch mixture – plain canary seed, panicum and yellow millets – together with spray millet, seeding grasses and some fine insectivorous mixture. They must also have a daily 'ration' of live food – a few small mealworms or maggots together with any other insects which can be collected in the house or garden. Some green food should be provided; chickweed seems to be a favourite. Grit and cuttlefish bone must always be available.

Green Singing Finch (*Serinus mozambicus*) Tropical Africa

Description 115 mm (4½ in.). A pretty little songster which, with care, may live for up to 20 years in an aviary. Crown greyish, merging with greenish grey of neck and back; chin, throat and under surfaces yellow; wings and tail black, some feathers edged with yellow; bright yellow markings above and below the eye; black eye stripe. Bill and legs horn-coloured. Females are very similar but can usually be distinguished by a necklace of rather indistinct black spots encircling the throat.

General Management These hardy little birds have been great favourites with aviculturists for many years. Males are sometimes inclined to be pugnacious with other birds; pairs get on well together but may indulge in some minor bickering outside the breeding season.

They need only a small aviary. Some vegetation is desirable to provide likely nest sites. If kept in aviaries throughout the year an unheated shelter must be provided.

Breeding Sometimes they nest in a tree or shrub; at other times they make use of a box or basket. Incubation is undertaken by the female. The chicks hatch out after 13 days.

In addition to their normal seed diet, provide sprouted seeds, soft food and increased supplies of greenstuff when nestlings are being fed. Occasional small items of live food may be taken whilst breeding and if ant pupae or wasp grubs are available they should be offered.

Feeding Plain canary seed, yellow panicum and spray millets provide the essentials of the bird's diet. Green food should be supplied regularly and many birds appreciate a slice of apple to pick at. Grit and cuttlefish bone should be available.

Wild Canary (*Serinus canarius*)
Canary Islands and Madeira

Description 140 mm (5½ in.). It is difficult to recognise this rather insignificant-looking little bird as the ancestor of the immense range of fancy canaries which have been developed. Upper surfaces yellow-olive with darker striations; underparts yellowish; wing and tail feathers black edged with yellowish green. Bill lead-coloured; legs dark horn.
The sexes are alike.

General Management Wild Canaries are nervous little birds. Ideally they should have a small aviary to themselves; they like plenty of natural cover.
When first received they should be acclimatised with just as much care as other seedeaters. Eventually they become hardy and can be wintered outside without heated quarters.

Breeding By no means easy to breed under controlled conditions, Wild Canaries may need a full year to settle down before there can be any real prospect of breeding success. Provide one or two wicker nest-baskets, plenty of suitable nesting material (hay, dry grass, rootlets, etc.), and disturb the pair as little as possible.
Sprouted seeds, extra green food and some insectile mixture should be provided when youngsters are being reared.

Feeding Plain canary seed, millets and a mixture of wild seeds suit these birds. They should also have seeding grasses and various green foods – chickweed, dandelion, groundsel, etc. Grit and cuttlefish bone must always be available.

Yellow-rumped Serin (*Serinus angolensis*) Tropical Africa

Description 140 mm (5½ in.). Rather soberly coloured but attractive little aviary birds and good songsters. Mainly grey in colour with darker striations; rump yellow. Bill and legs horn-coloured.

The sexes are similar.

General Management Hardy and easily managed, Yellow-rumped Serins, like the related Grey Singing Finch, are not widely kept by aviculturists; probably their rather drab plumage is the reason for this. But they are worth a place in any collection of small seedeaters and males have a pleasant song. They can prove to be rather aggressive and a breeding pair should be housed alone.

Breeding These little birds are extremely difficult to sex and the male's song is the best guide. It is worth while obtaining three or four birds from which to select a pair.

They will make use of either a box or wicker nest-basket. The eggs hatch after about 14 days and the chicks leave the nest about three weeks later. The parents should be given some live food and sprouted seeds when they are rearing young.

Feeding A mixture of small plain canary seed, yellow and panicum millets; also seeding grasses and an occasional millet spray. Green food should always be provided and some birds learn to enjoy pecking at a slice of apple. Grit and cuttlefish bone are essential.

Rufous-collared Sparrow (*Zonotrichia capensis*)
Central and South America

Description 150 mm (6 in.). Attractive little birds with a pleasant song. They become hardy and are excellent for a garden aviary. Back and upper surfaces brown with darker striations; collar and neck rufous-orange; Throat white with black markings forming a necklace; breast and underparts grey-white; crown grey with black stripes; white eyebrow stripe; black eye streak. Bill brown; legs flesh-coloured.
The sexes are alike.

General Management These birds are not difficult to acclimatise. They can eventually be kept outdoors throughout the year but should be provided with a frost-free shelter.
They can be housed with other finches but a potential breeding pair should be given a small aviary to themselves.

Breeding A pair of these attractive little birds may breed in a suitable small aviary. They should have ample natural cover and one or two wicker nest-baskets from which to make a choice of nest site. Sprouted seeds and extra live food should be supplied if young are to be reared successfully.

Feeding Rufous-collared Sparrows should be given a mixed seed diet which includes plain canary seed, white and yellow millets. Seeding grass heads and sprouted seeds can be offered from time to time. They also enjoy picking through an insectile mixture and mixed wild seeds. They should always have grit and cuttlefish bone.

Yellow Sparrow (*Auripasser luteus*) Eastern Africa
Golden Sparrow, Sudan Golden Sparrow, Golden Song Sparrow

Description 130 mm (5 in.). A gaily coloured little sparrow which is easy to keep and hardy. Head, neck and under surfaces bright yellow; back chestnut; wings and tail brown. Bill black during the breeding season; at other times horn-coloured. Legs are brown.
Females have the head and upper surfaces buff-brown; underparts buff-yellow.

General Management Yellow Sparrows are easily acclimatised and can be wintered outside. Dry sleeping accommodation is essential.
Although active little birds they tend not to show up in a natural aviary, preferring to spend most of their time hidden in the vegetation.
They are inclined to be aggressive and will chase smaller companions such as waxbills and other small finches. They are good companions for some of the smaller weavers, mannikins and Java Sparrows.

Breeding Although widely kept by aviculturists, the Yellow Sparrow has bred only infrequently in aviaries. A pair should have a small aviary to themselves. Provide plenty of cover; thickets of gorse are good and bunches of this prickly but easily obtained cover can be wired into place to provide temporary nest sites. Wicker nest-baskets can be placed well down in this cover as an encouragement to building.
If chicks are hatched out, additional foods including sprouted seeds, seeding grasses and plenty of small insect life should be provided.
Yellow Sparrows will not tolerate disturbance once nesting operations are under way and the aviculturist must curb natural curiosity at this particular time – otherwise breeding will almost certainly be abandoned.

Feeding These little birds are very easy to feed. Although they thrive on a staple diet of plain canary seed and millet, they will be healthier and happier if given additional millet sprays, green food and some live food. The birds enjoy an occasional caterpillar or mealworm, although the latter is not essential outside the breeding season. Grit and cuttlefish bone must always be available.

Magpie Mannikin (*Amauresthes fringilloides*)
West and East Africa

Description 130 mm (5 in.). One of the larger mannikins. Head and throat glossy black; back, wings and tail brown; under surfaces white; some darker markings on the flanks. Bill, upper mandible black, lower light horn; legs black.

The sexes are alike.

General Management These handsome birds are much less frequently available than most other Indian and African mannikins.

Acclimatised birds live well in aviaries; they become very hardy and can be wintered outside without heat. A look at their formidable beak gives a clear indication that their companions should be chosen with care. While not especially aggressive they are capable of defending themselves in mixed company and it would be wise not to associate them with waxbills or any other birds of comparable size. They can be housed with birds such as Java Sparrows.

A pair are much safer housed alone, particularly if it is hoped to persuade them to nest successfully.

Breeding Selection of a true pair is often a problem. Females are said to have slightly more slender bills and small heads. It is sometimes possible to pick out a pair from a larger group, but positive identification of single birds, without others with which to make a comparison, is almost impossible.

If a true pair can be obtained they usually prove to be free breeders. They should have an aviary to themselves during the breeding season, plenty of cover and one or two wicker baskets, of the globular type, or open-fronted boxes.

Magpie Mannikins construct a substantial, bulky nest using small twigs, dried grasses, leaves and suchlike items. In the wild they build nests in colonies and it is possible that more than one pair could be housed in the same large aviary. Odd birds of either sex would have to be removed if the group were to have any chance of settling down to serious breeding.

Up to six eggs are laid and incubation is completed in about 12 days. The young are normally reared on seed with the addition of some sprouted seeds, millet sprays and small live food. In their natural habitat these birds are known to be fond of termites and one can assume that ant pupae would be a valuable food supplement during the breeding season.

Feeding Magpie Mannikins should be provided with a mixture of plain canary, white and yellow millets. They are fond of spray millet. Green food should be provided, although individual birds seem to vary in their willingness to eat anything other than a seed diet. Grit and cuttlefish bone must be supplied.

Indigo Bunting (*Passerina cyanea*) Eastern USA

Description 130 mm (5 in.). Handsome birds with distinctive colouring. Males have a pleasant song. In colour the male Indigo Bunting is mainly dark blue; head with violet suffusions; other areas of the plumage show a green sheen. Bill lead-coloured; legs black.

Females, and out-of-colour males, have the head and upper surfaces warm brown; underparts pale brown with some darker streaks.

General Management Indigo Buntings are hardy birds. They are at their best in a suitably planted garden aviary and can remain outside throughout the year. Like most related species, males can prove extremely aggressive when in breeding condition and if they are to be housed in a mixed aviary their companions should be chosen with care.

Newly obtained birds should not be housed outside until they have had a chance to become acclimatised.

Breeding Indigo Buntings are not particularly easy to breed, and to achieve success it is almost essential to provide the breeding pair with an aviary to themselves so that they have seclusion and plenty of natural cover. They need plenty of live food to rear their young successfully.

Feeding A staple diet consists of plain canary seed, white and yellow millets. They can also be given a wild seed mixture. Green food and some live insects should be offered at regular intervals. They must have grit and cuttlefish bone.

Versicolor Bunting (*Passerina versicolor*)
Southern USA, Mexico and Central America

Description 130 mm (5 in.). Less frequently available than most of the American buntings. Rather muted colours, but a very beautiful little bird. Forehead and chin black; front of crown, cheeks, nape and rump purplish blue; back of crown scarlet; back, breast and under surfaces mainly chestnut-purple. Bill and legs horn-coloured.
Females are mainly dull brown in colour with paler underparts.

General Management The Versicolor Bunting is regarded as rather more delicate than related species and many authorities advocate heated quarters during winter. It is difficult to understand why recommendations of this kind are made. The species, when acclimatised, will prove quite capable of wintering in an outdoor aviary, provided it is not exposed to wet or damp conditions.

Breeding The Versicolor Bunting has proved to be as reluctant to breed in aviaries as most of its relatives. A small planted flight should be allocated to the pair. Furnishings can be similar to those recommended for the Nonpareil Bunting. Plenty of small live insects will be required if chicks are hatched out.

Feeding Versicolor Buntings are not difficult to feed. They should be given a seed mixture which includes plain canary seed, yellow and panicum millets. To provide more variety a wild seed mixture can be offered from time to time. They also like seeding grasses, greenstuff and live food. Two or three mealworms or maggots can be provided; during the summer offer more natural items such as caterpillars, small grasshoppers, etc. Supplies of grit and cuttlefish bone must always be available.

Rainbow Bunting (*Passerina leclancheri*) Mexico

Description 140 mm ($5\frac{1}{2}$ in.). Charming little birds but not easy to establish in aviaries. Upper surfaces glossy sky-blue with a tinge of green on the upper back; forehead and crown green; nape and sides of neck cobalt-blue; underparts orange-yellow, brightest on the throat and upper breast. Bill and legs grey-black.

Females have olive-green upper surfaces and paler yellowish-green underparts. There is usually a small amount of blue in the female's wing and tail feathers.

General Management The Rainbow Bunting is a particularly difficult species to acclimatise, and even when this has been successfully accomplished the birds frequently prove to be more delicate than many authorities suggest.

They seem to be poor travellers and hence newly obtained birds need careful handling and to be kept warm if they are to survive. Eventually they can be put into an outdoor aviary. Once established the Rainbow Bunting can be kept outside throughout the year as long as it has access to frost-free quarters. Wet or damp conditions will prove much more troublesome than low temperatures.

Breeding These birds have proved themselves extremely reluctant breeders in a controlled environment. The best chance of success will be with an established pair housed in a densely planted aviary and with protection from driving winds and rain. Provide them with plenty of natural and artificial nest sites. Like related species they usually build fairly low down in a bush or thicket.

If eggs are hatched an abundance of live food is essential for the successful rearing of chicks. These and other buntings are best treated as one would a pair of insectivorous softbills at this time and no effort should be spared to provide a varied and constant supply of small insects. Rainbow Buntings are quite adept at capturing flies and the like; a piece of raw meat or fish hung in the flight will attract a great deal of useful food.

Feeding A mixture of plain canary seed, white, yellow and panicum millets should be supplemented with seeding grasses, sprouted seeds and various items of greenstuff – chickweed, groundsel and so on. Live food is essential at all times. This species frequently ignores other foods in preference to mealworms if given the opportunity. Although valuable, particularly during the colder months of the year when little natural live food is available, the supply of mealworms should be carefully regulated – not more than two or three per bird each day.

Some Rainbow Buntings can be persuaded to take small quantities of insectivorous mixture if one or two maggots are mixed into it. This is a useful addition to diet, but moderation is again essential. Grit and cuttlefish bone should always be available.

Buntings The subfamily of New World seedeaters, Fringillinae, are called buntings in Europe Europe and sparrows in America. They are the largest and most widespread of all the seed-eater groups, containing some 266 species. In the wild they prefer a habitat of grassland, scrubland and open woodland, where they forage close to the ground for seeds. Some take a little vegetable matter and insects but most require plentiful supplies of insects for feeding their young. All build open cup-shaped nests fairly close to the ground.

Nonpareil Bunting (*Passerina ciris*) Southern USA
Painted Bunting

Description 140 mm (5½ in.). An extremely beautiful little seedeater, especially in the wild. Unfortunately some of the male's brilliant colours fade when the species is kept under controlled conditions. Head, nape and shoulders bright blue; back, wings and tail green – with some red feathers in the latter; rump orange; under surfaces vermilion. Bill and legs horn colour.

Females are much duller. The upper parts are grey-green; under surfaces dull yellow.

General Management Nonpareil Buntings have enjoyed great popularity for many years. Even when housed in near-natural conditions in a garden aviary and provided with a variety of live foods, the male's brilliant red under surfaces fade to orange and eventually even to a drab yellow. The careful use of colour food may do something to remedy the problem.

Provided their sleeping quarters are dry, acclimatised Nonpareil Buntings are quite capable of wintering outside without heat.

Breeding The Nonpareil Bunting has been bred only on rare occasions in confinement. Despite this, it is probably incorrect to classify the species as a 'difficult' breeder. On the occasions when a pair has settled down to nesting in an aviary they have usually proved to be extremely prolific. It is possible that the shortage of females may be one of the main reasons why so few successes have been recorded.

A quiet and secluded aviary with one or two dense thickets to provide suitable nest sites is the most suitable environment for a pair of these handsome birds.

They may use a nest-box or wicker basket. Alternatively they can be given an old cup-shaped nest. Plenty of suitable building materials should be provided. Grass, rootlets and strands of dry sphagnum moss are often used in the construction of their nest.

Incubation lasts 14 days and is undertaken by the female. Both parents feed the chicks and it is vital that plenty of live food is available.

Feeding Although plain canary seed and millet provide a basic diet, it is essential they are given regular supplies of live food. Outside the breeding season they need little more than two or three mealworms or cleaned maggots each day; spiders, flies, grasshoppers and so on can be given to provide variety, but they are by no means essential.

Greenstuff should be offered, together with seeding grasses. Grit and cuttlefish bone must be available at all times.

Lazuli Bunting (*Passerina amoena*)

Eastern USA and Mexico

Description 130 mm (5 in.). Lacking the brilliant colours of some of its close relatives, this is nevertheless an attractive species. Head, shoulders and rump bright blue; back, wings and tail slate-blue; breast pale chestnut shading to white on the abdomen. Bill and legs black. The female has dull-brown upper surfaces; breast and underparts warm buff. There is a faint wash of slate-blue on the head.

General Management Lazuli Buntings are not difficult to acclimatise. They should be housed indoors in a roomy cage or flight until they have settled down and adjusted to any change in climate. Once acclimatised they can be housed in a garden aviary. They will winter out of doors without heat, provided attention is paid to the need for a dry shelter. If possible, the birds will probably be better roosting inside their shelter during periods of really severe weather.

In a planted aviary these birds are much more likely to show themselves than the Rainbow Bunting. Males frequently perch on a high branch to utter their pleasantly varied little song.

Breeding Few breeding successes have been recorded with this species. There seems no reason, given good aviary accommodation and a suitable diet, why a pair of Lazuli Buntings should not be persuaded to nest and rear young in a controlled environment.

They should be housed in a thickly planted flight, with plenty of low-growing shrubs and other vegetation providing the sort of cover these buntings use in a wild state. Needless to say, the chances of success will be greatly enhanced if the birds have an aviary to themselves. Like other buntings they are highly insectivorous during the breeding season and must be provided with a plentiful supply of live insects. If chicks are hatched out they will be fed almost exclusively on live food until they are fledged.

Feeding A varied seed diet including plain canary seed and millets provides much of the Lazuli Buntings' needs outside the breeding season. They should also be given sprouted seeds, greenstuff and various items of live food. Some will take a little fruit. Grit and cuttlefish bone must be provided.

Ringed Warbling Finch (*Poospiza torquata*)
Western South America

Description 130 mm (5 in.). Quietly coloured but handsome little birds. They soon become hardy and thrive in garden aviaries. Upper surfaces dark grey-brown; throat white; underparts grey-white; head and prominent eye stripe black. Bill dark horn; legs flesh-coloured. Females lack the distinctive black head and eye stripe.

General Management These very attractive little birds are now more readily available and make excellent aviary subjects. Although newly obtained birds need as much care as other species they settle down quickly and eventually are hardy enough to remain out of doors throughout the year.

They are best housed in a planted garden aviary. Warbling Finches are active and rather 'tit-like' in habit. They seem not to be particularly aggressive and can be housed with other similar-sized birds although, as with most species, if breeding is to be successfully accomplished they are far better given a small flight to themselves.

Their aviary should be furnished with plenty of bushes and thickets of vegetation. They are rarely still and spend most of their time investigating leaves and branches for insects. They can prove to be surprisingly acrobatic and will often hunt through patches of vegetation in much the same manner as tits.

Breeding Although they lack any bright colours, these are interesting little birds which are well worth attention as breeding subjects. Given a small flight to themselves a pair may make use of a wicker nest-basket fixed securely in place in the depths of a bush.

If chicks are hatched out a varied diet, including a high proportion of live food, is essential. The parents should also be supplied with items of green food, sprouted seeds, seeding grasses, etc.

Feeding Although they can be kept on a diet of seed alone, warbling finches are quite insectivorous and a much more varied menu is desirable. They should have a mixture of plain canary seed and millets; they also enjoy picking through a wild seed mixture. Live food should always be supplied – maggots and mealworms will suffice. A small quantity of insectivorous food should be given each day together with fruit. They must always have access to grit and cuttlefish bone.

Golden-breasted Bunting (*Emberiza flaviventris*)
Africa south of the Sahara

Description 165 mm (6½ in.). Upper surfaces chestnut-brown; breast bright yellow, tinged with red in the centre; rump grey-brown; abdomen whitish; wings black with white bars; tail black with white. Bill black; legs flesh-coloured.

The female is similar but rather less brightly coloured.

General Management These birds are excellent aviary subjects. Handsomely marked and brightly coloured, they are not difficult to acclimatise. They can be wintered in an outdoor aviary but will not tolerate damp conditions. They are an attractive sight in a planted aviary – active and showing up well against the foliage.

Unfortunately they are not as freely available as many other African seedeaters. This is undoubtedly a species with which aviculturists should persevere in efforts to establish aviary-bred strains.

Breeding Like all buntings they are somewhat nervous and highly strung. Breeding is more likely if they are housed in a secluded, planted aviary where other birds are not likely to disturb them.

The nest is usually built in a bush just a few feet above the ground. It is a cup-shaped structure and constructed of rootlets, grass, etc. Two or three eggs are laid. Incubation lasts for 13 days and the chicks leave the nest about three weeks later.

In common with other members of the family, this species is highly insectivorous during the breeding season and an abundant supply of small live food is required if chicks are to be reared successfully. Small, cleaned maggots usually provide the mainstay but other items should be collected from the garden.

Sprouted seeds and seeding grasses should also be provided.

Feeding Mainly plain canary seed and millets, including spray millet, with regular supplies of green food and live insects. A few maggots should be given each day. In a planted aviary the birds will succeed in capturing a wide variety of other insects but they need increased supplies as the breeding season approaches.

They should also be given seeding grasses and other items of green food gathered from the garden and hedgerows. On this point, do bear in mind the need to be absolutely certain that items of natural food are gathered and used only if there is certain knowledge that they have not been contaminated with any of the toxic sprays now commonly used.

Virginian Cardinal (*Richmondena cardinalis*)
USA and Mexico
Virginian Nightingale, Red Cardinal

Description 230 mm (9 in.). Strikingly beautiful birds in the wild. Unfortunately they lose some
of their brilliance with successive moults in confinement. Entire plumage scarlet except
wings which are brownish red; face, chin and an area round the base of the bill black.
Bill red; legs brown.

The female is mainly brown in colour with lighter underparts.

General Management Although an alternative name for this bird is Virginian Nightingale, it is
perhaps more optimistic than accurate. Males have a powerful 'voice' and often sing well
into the night, but they are by no means among the world's great feathered musicians.

A pair of Virginian Cardinals should have an aviary to themselves. They are hardy and do
not require heat during the colder months of the year. A dry shelter should be available
during really severe weather.

Breeding Provide one or two open-fronted boxes. They should be placed fairly high up in the
flight and screened with suitable cover.

The two or three eggs are incubated by the female for 14 days. The chicks are fed on a diet
consisting almost exclusively of insects, and a supply of maggots, mealworms, small grasshoppers, woodlice, smooth caterpillars, etc. is essential.

Feeding These birds need a varied diet including plain canary seed, millets, hemp, some sunflower, buckwheat, etc. They also enjoy green food and some fruit. Some live food should
always be provided. Grit and cuttlefish bone are essential.

Pope Cardinal (*Paroaria dominicana*) Eastern Brazil
Dominican Cardinal

Description 180 mm (7 in.). A very handsome cardinal. Head and throat bright red; neck and under surfaces white, greyer on the abdomen; back, wings and tail dark grey. Bill horn-coloured; legs dark grey. The sexes are alike.

General Management Pope Cardinals are excellent aviary birds, their distinctive plumage showing well in a planted flight. They quickly become acclimatised and extremely hardy, well able to winter in an outside aviary without heat. They should have a fairly large aviary with plenty of cover. They can be housed with other birds of comparable size and temperament but breeding is unlikely unless a pair are given their own aviary.

Like most other cardinals they are inclined to remain nervous and breeding accommodation should be as secluded as possible. They seem to prefer to roost in an outside flight, even in winter, and some form of protection should be fixed above favourite roosting spots.

Breeding This species may make use of a nest-basket or box, or build its cup-shaped nest in a bush above the ground. The chicks are reared almost exclusively on live food to begin with and the parents should be supplied with ant pupae, grasshoppers, small locusts, cleaned maggots, etc. Later during the fledgling period some sprouted seeds can be provided.

Feeding Plain canary seed, white and yellow millets provide a basic diet for these birds. In addition they can be given occasional small quantities of sunflower and hemp. Green food should be offered frequently and some birds acquire a liking for fruit. Live food, although not essential outside the breeding season, can be provided in the form of two or three maggots or mealworms each day. Grit and cuttlefish bone must always be supplied.

Green Cardinal (*Gubernatrix cristata*)

Brazil and Argentina

Yellow Cardinal

Description 190 mm (7½ in.). A soberly coloured species; and a fairly free breeder in aviaries. Upper surfaces olive-green with darker markings; cheeks and throat yellow; crest and a bib-like patch on the throat black; underparts greenish yellow. Bill greyish-horn; legs dark grey. Females are much duller, with most of the green and yellow of the male's plumage replaced by areas of grey-green and dull white.

General Management Green Cardinals can be housed in a moderately sized garden aviary. They are hardy birds and do not require heat during the winter months. Although they are often described as less hardy than other cardinals they do not appear susceptible to low temperatures. They are much less happy in damp conditions, however, and do not really thrive if they have to endure a cold, damp winter without access to a comfortable shelter.

They can be housed with other birds of similar size outside the breeding season: weavers, whydahs, Java Sparrows and so on make good companions. Odd birds do not normally cause trouble in mixed company but pairs should always be regarded as somewhat suspect.

Breeding An established pair of Green Cardinals, housed alone in a planted garden aviary, will usually prove to be free breeders. They like to build a nest in fairly thick cover, usually a bush or shrub. Some pairs will make use of an open-fronted box or nest-basket; alternatively an old medium-sized, cup-shaped nest may have more appeal.

Like many other seedeating species they feed their young to a great extent on insects – at least during the first two or three weeks. Maggots and mealworms can be used in moderation; small locusts and grasshoppers are valuable, together with caterpillars, woodlice, spiders, ant pupae and wasp grubs. In addition to their normal seed diet they should also have some sprouted seeds and seeding grass heads at this time. Some pairs will take insectivorous food during the breeding season.

The youngsters should be removed to another aviary as soon as they are seen to be able to fend for themselves, usually within a couple of weeks of leaving the nest when they are about one month old. Their parents should start on a second nest and their first offspring may come in for some rough handling from the male if left to share the breeding aviary.

Feeding Green Cardinals are not difficult to feed and can be kept in good condition on a mixed seed diet with regular supplies of green food and an occasional mealworm.

But, as with other species, diet should be regarded for its long-term effects not only in keeping birds alive and in apparent good order but also as a means of inducing breeding condition at the right season. A simple and somewhat spartan seed diet, which may seem to be all that is required to keep birds fit, is unlikely to produce birds capable of nesting successfully.

In addition to a seed mixture which should include plain canary, white and yellow millets, hemp and sunflower seeds (the last two being offered in moderation), Green Cardinals should have various green foods including groundsel, coltsfoot, dandelion, chickweed and so on. Earlier in the year they should be supplied with fresh branches of fruit trees in bud.

Live food is not essential except when the birds are breeding, but they will benefit from occasional tit-bits – mealworms, small locusts, etc. They must always have access to grit and cuttlefish bone.

Japanese Hawfinch (*Eophona personata*)

Japan westwards through Central Asia

Black-headed Hawfinch, Japanese Grosbeak

Description 200 mm (8 in.). Large and handsome seedeaters which are occasionally available to aviculturists. They are not difficult to keep and, once established, are invariably seen in impeccable plumage. Head and throat glossy black; collar blue-grey; back vinous; under surfaces rufous-brown; rump white; wings black with white bar; tail black. Bill mainly yellow, pale mauve at base and with black markings at tip; legs flesh-coloured.

Females are less brightly coloured; the head and throat are grey. Bill yellow.

General Management Like other hawfinches, these birds have heavy, workmanlike bills and give every appearance of being well able to take care of themselves in mixed company! In fact they are not normally as aggressive as their appearance might suggest.

They are extremely hardy birds and, although they may be a little nervous to begin with, soon settle down to aviary conditions. A planted garden aviary which provides some thickets of evergreen in which to roost suits these birds admirably, as they do not require heated quarters.

Breeding A true pair is a worthwhile acquisition and they would certainly merit a suitable aviary in which they might be induced to breed.

A wicker nest-basket fixed securely into a suitable bush or thicket of evergreen might interest them; alternatively they will construct a nest in a similar situation.

The clutch of up to four eggs will be incubated by the female for two weeks.

Plenty of small live food, extra greenstuff and some canary rearing food should be supplied when youngsters are in the nest. While maggots and mealworms will be accepted, efforts should be made to provide small smooth caterpillars, ant pupae and so forth.

Feeding A suitable staple diet for these birds should include plain canary seed, buckwheat, hemp, sunflower, etc. The last two should be given sparingly. Green food should be offered regularly, together with occasional items of live food. Grit and cuttlefish bone should always be available.

Hawfinches are found from Europe through to eastern Asia. In Europe the bird is named for its liking of seeds from the hawthorn. In Asia the Hawfinch is replaced by the Japanese Hawfinch, or Japanese Grosbeak as it is called there.

Pagoda Mynah (*Sturnus pagodarum*) India and Ceylon
Pagoda Starling, Brahminy Mynah

Description 200 mm (8 in.). Head and crest black; face, neck and under surfaces rich buff; upper parts grey-blue; outer flight feathers of wings black; tail dark brown with white tip. Bill yellow, with blue at base; legs greenish yellow.

The sexes are very similar.

General Management One of a number of Asiatic starlings which are regularly kept as aviary birds. These birds become hardy and can be wintered outside. Newly imported birds need a period of acclimatisation.

Their behaviour is typical of most starlings; in an aviary they are confident and somewhat aggressive. This impression is somewhat enhanced by their rather swaggering gait. Although a single bird can be housed with other softbills of similar size, a pair should be given an aviary to themselves. They do not need a lot of space and usually become tame very quickly.

Breeding Pagoda Mynahs will make use of a large box or log in which to construct their large, rather untidy nest. Sometimes they build on a shelf inside the shelter.

They need plenty of live food if young are to be reared successfully. Locusts and grasshoppers are valuable, but mealworms and maggots can supply the bulk of their needs.

Feeding These omnivorous birds can be given a variety of foods, including a coarse-grade insectile mixture, various fruits and live food. They are fond of berries and also enjoy soaked raisins and sultanas. Some finely scraped raw beef can be mixed with their food from time to time.

Hill Mynah (*Gracula religiosa*) Southern Asia
Indian Grackle

Description 330 mm (13 in.). Several geographical forms are recognised. They vary mainly in size between 250 mm (10 in.) and 380 mm (15 in.), and also in the size and shape of the wattles. Almost entirely glossy black, with green and purple sheen; wattles of bare skin on sides of face and nape yellow. Bill and legs orange.
The sexes are alike.

General Management The aviculturist whose interest lies in breeding these birds will be well advised to start off with young birds. Since adults usually remain wild when captured they are totally unsuited to life in small aviaries.

Once acclimatised, Hill Mynahs are extremely hardy and can be housed outdoors throughout the year, provided they have a comfortable, dry shelter.

Breeding A pair of Hill Mynahs should be housed in a spacious aviary and provided with a box or large log in which to build their nest.

Plenty of live food is required to rear the young; grasshoppers and locusts are excellent. These large grackles will also make use of baby mice, frogs and newts as rearing food.

Feeding Although pet mynahs seem to thrive on a proprietary food mixture, potential breeding stock should have a much more varied diet which includes a coarse-grade insectile food, mixed fruits and plenty of live insects.

Malabar Mynah (*Sturnus malabaricus*)
India and the Himalayas
Grey-headed Mynah

Description 200 mm (8 in.). An attractive species which thrives in a garden aviary. Head and neck light grey. Some of the feathers are elongated and have lighter shafts giving a frosted appearance; back and upper surfaces dark grey; entire under surfaces pale rufous; primaries and tail dark brown. Bill green with blue at base and yellow tip; legs buff-brown.
The sexes are alike.

General Management Although frequently kept and easily managed, the Malabar Mynah is by no means one of the aviculturist's favourites. Perhaps the fact that the birds are not so exotic-looking as other mynah species, coupled with their rather domineering nature, may have something to do with their lack of popularity.

Newly taken birds settle down quickly and after a short period of acclimatisation become very hardy. They are not especially dangerous in mixed company but tend to assert themselves strongly over such matters as a favourite roosting spot or first use of the bath. Their attitude is typical of most starlings rather swashbuckling approach to life.

Breeding This is another species where one of the first obstacles to overcome in successful breeding is the acquisition of a true pair. It is almost impossible to differentiate between male and female and the only reliable guide is the behaviour of individual birds.

Given an aviary to themselves, a pair of Malabar Mynahs will usually breed successfully. They build their nest in a box or hollow log. Up to five eggs are laid and incubation lasts for two weeks. Supplies of live food must be stepped up when the eggs hatch. As the chicks grow and increasing quantities of insects are required, it is usually necessary to supplement the supply of mealworms and maggots with such things as locusts, grasshoppers, woodlice and so on. Some fruit and soft food should also be fed to the young birds.

Feeding Malabar Mynahs are easily fed. In addition to a coarse-grade insectile food they should have plenty of fruit: apples, pears, grapes, sweet oranges, soaked raisins and sultanas, and various berries. Some live food is also essential but the birds will be quite happy with a small daily ration of mealworms or maggots.

Spreo Starling (*Spreo superbus*) East Africa
Superb Starling

Description 200 mm (8 in.). One of the best-known and most beautiful of the glossy starlings. Head, neck and upper breast blue, darker on the head; back and upper surfaces green; lower breast and belly bright chestnut, separated from the blue of the upper breast by a broad band of white. The entire plumage of the upper surfaces and breast has a brilliant iridescent sheen. Bill and legs black.

The sexes are alike.

General Management Easily managed and hardy, Spreo Starlings should be housed in a roomy, planted aviary. Although hardy enough to winter outside they should have adequate protection from driving winds and rain. They seem to prefer an outside roosting place and once the favourite spot is identified it should be covered with a piece of rigid polythene or some light boarding so the birds do not become soaked and chilled during heavy rain.

While single birds can be housed in a mixed group of similar-sized softbills, a mated pair of Spreo Starlings must have an aviary to themselves. Like most starlings they are confident, aggressive birds; when in breeding condition they can be positively murderous!

Breeding These starlings will use a large nest-box with a suitable entrance hole near the top. Provide them with plenty of building material – hay, rootlets, dried grass, etc. – for they build a large and somewhat untidy nest which usually fills the box completely.

The three or four eggs hatch after an incubation period of 13 days. The adults need plenty of live food when they have young to rear. Mealworms and maggots can be used to supplement caterpillars, woodlice and whatever else can be collected in and around the garden. Locusts are an excellent food and the young 'hoppers' are extremely valuable for feeding to the young of these and similar-sized birds.

The youngsters should be removed to another aviary as soon as they are seen to be self-supporting. If left in the breeding flight there is every possibility they will be attacked by their parents should the old birds decide to nest for a second time.

Feeding Virtually omnivorous, Spreo Starlings should have a coarse-grade insectile mixture with plenty of fruit and a daily ration of live food. Fruit – apples, pears, grapes and so on – is best chopped into small cubes. These birds are very fond of berries and will eat both wild and cultivated types.

Small amounts of minced raw beef should be added to the insectile mixture two or three times a week.

Purple Glossy Starling (*Lamprotornis purpureus*)
West and Central Africa
Purple-headed Glossy Starling, Purple Starling

Description 230 mm (9 in.). One of the best-known of the glossy starlings and a popular aviary bird. The plumage is essentially dark blue with deep violet, purple and green highlights; eyes bright yellow. Bill and legs black.

The sexes are alike.

General Management Glossy starlings are among the easiest of the larger softbills to acclimatise They become hardy enough to winter outside without heat but need a comfortable, dry shed in which to roost.

They are active birds and should be given as large an aviary as possible. They are not trustworthy in mixed company except with birds of comparable size and temperament such as jay-thrushes, the larger weavers and whydahs, etc. A true pair must always be housed alone. To appreciate the full beauty of these birds, they need a spacious, sunny aviary. They spend a good deal of their time on the wing, flying from end to end in their flight and making good use of available space.

Breeding Most of the glossy starlings will make use of a roomy wooden box for nesting purposes; something measuring about 300 mm (12 in.) square will suffice; an entrance hole near the top should be provided. The nest itself is usually a bulky structure and ample material should be provided. The two or three eggs hatch after an incubation period of about two weeks and the chicks remain in the nest for a further month.

The adults need plenty of fruit and suitable live food when chicks are being reared. Small locusts, grasshoppers, smooth caterpillars, mealworms and maggots should be offered. The youngsters should be removed to another aviary as soon as they are seen to be self-supporting.

Feeding Although fruit – diced apples, pears, grapes, bananas, etc. – provides much of their diet, glossy starlings must also have a coarse-grade insectile mixture and regular supplies of live food. Minced beef can be added to the insectile food from time to time.

They will take maggots, mealworms and various items of live food gathered in the garden. Green food can be offered but is rarely taken.

Bananaquit (*Coereba flaveola*)
Northern South America, Central America and the Caribbean

Description 115 mm (4½ in.). Attractive little birds with rather 'tit-like' habits. They are usually tame and confiding. Head, upper surfaces, chin and throat black; lower breast yellow, shading into whitish on abdomen; distinctive white eyebrow stripe; tail black tipped with white. Bill and legs black.

Females are similar but with less brightly coloured underparts.

General Management Ideal occupants of a conservatory or a sheltered garden aviary. In either situation plenty of tall-growing plants are advisable; Bananaquits are active little birds and spend a great deal of time moving through foliage in search of small insects. They are probably better given roomy indoor quarters for the winter months.

Breeding Breeding is more likely to take place in a planted conservatory than a garden aviary. The birds nest fairly low down in suitable vegetation and build a globular nest. Two or three eggs are laid and incubation – carried out by the female – lasts for 13 days.

Sponge cake soaked in a nectar mixture together with fruit flies will be used to feed the nestlings. Some insectile food and soft fruit should also be provided.

Feeding These birds should not be allowed to consume nectar *ad lib*. It is essential they have a more varied diet. Sponge cake soaked in honey water, sweet oranges, grapes, pears, a fine-grade insectivorous food and various items of small live food will suit them well. Despite their common name they are in no way addicted to bananas, although these can be offered, in moderation, together with other fruits.

Yellow-winged Sugarbird (*Cyanerpes cyaneus*)
Southern Mexico to Brazil and Bolivia

Description 115 mm (4½ in.). The male, in breeding plumage, is a brilliant little gem. Mainly bright purplish blue; back, wings, tail and lores black; crown iridescent turquoise-blue; undersides of flight feathers yellow. Bill black; legs red.

Females are olive-green in colour, lighter on the under surfaces, and with paler yellow webs on the undersides of the wings. Bill black; legs flesh-brown.

Males undergo a period of eclipse plumage when they resemble the females. The sexes can always be distinguished by the male's coral-red legs.

General Management These birds adapt quickly to aviary life and will live for many years in an outdoor aviary when acclimatised. A suitably adapted greenhouse or conservatory also provides good accommodation for them.

Breeding Plenty of cover should be provided in the breeding aviary – which need not be a very large structure. Success is more likely if they do not have to compete with other birds in the same quarters.

The nest is built of rootlets and similar materials. Usually two eggs are laid and incubation, usually by the female, lasts 12 days. The nestlings are fed on soft fruits and tiny insects.

Feeding Sugarbirds do well on a diet of soft fruit and sponge cake soaked in honey water. They should also have a daily allowance of small live food. Mealworms and maggots are a useful standby but spiders, small flying insects and tiny smooth caterpillars should be given whenever possible. In a naturally planted aviary these birds will capture a good deal of live food themselves.

Blue-capped Tanager (*Thraupis cyanocephala*)

North-western areas of South America

Blue-headed Tanager

Description 190 mm (7½ in.). One of the larger tanagers. Acclimatised birds live well in outdoor aviaries. Top and sides of head cobalt-blue; back, wings and tail black, the wing feathers with olive-green margins; under surfaces dark blue; shoulders golden green; forehead and eye streak black; rump yellow. Bill black; legs dark horn-coloured.

The sexes are alike.

General Management Like the related Palm and Silver-blue Tanagers, this species, when acclimatised, is not difficult to maintain in good health and becomes surprisingly hardy.

These tanagers look most attractive in a planted garden aviary where, if provided with comfortable winter accommodation, they are more likely to thrive over a long period than if housed in a greenhouse or conservatory.

A frost-free shelter is desirable during the colder months of the year and it may be wise to keep the birds inside during periods of severe weather. On the other hand, the related Silver-blue has been known to survive successive winters in a shelterless garden aviary. The bird simply refused to be caught for transfer to more comfortable quarters and was the very picture of health throughout his near four years out of doors. He roosted in an evergreen bush and appeared to be untroubled by rain, hail, snow, frost and fog!

Although this is another species one would hesitate to label aggressive, it is necessary to exercise care in housing them with companions, and a known true pair should always have an aviary to themselves.

These tanagers are extremely fond of bathing and should have free access to a bath.

Breeding Secluded, planted accommodation is essential if these birds are to breed successfully in an aviary. They should be provided with plenty of cover, including some fairly tall-growing bushes or strong climbing plants in which one or two wicker nest-baskets can be fixed. These tanagers build an open cup-shaped nest of rootlets and dry grass. In the wild they sometimes make use of cobwebs to line the finished structure.

Usually two eggs are laid. Incubation is carried out by the female for approximately 14 days. Both parents feed the nestlings, which may remain in the nest for between three and four weeks.

The parents must have plenty of insects at this time. They feed the youngsters on small smooth caterpillars, spiders, flies, grasshoppers, etc. Among other foods which can be offered while chicks are being fed are soft fruit, sponge cake soaked in honey water, and any berries that are in season.

Feeding Blue-capped Tanagers should be offered a variety of soft fruits, including apple, pear, sweet orange, grapes, etc. They are also fond of berries. A fine-grade insectile mixture should be given from time to time; small quantities sprinkled on a piece of fruit will often induce the birds to try what is, to them, a somewhat synthetic item of diet. They are fond of sponge cake soaked in an artificial nectar mixture, but should not be allowed to consume this to the exclusion of other foods.

Live food should be offered at all times. Small soft-bodied insects such as green caterpillars, grasshoppers, spiders, etc. are easily gathered from the garden during the summer months. In winter the aviculturist will probably have to resort to cleaned maggots and small mealworms. Up to half a dozen of each can be given each day.

Blue-shouldered Mountain Tanager (*Compsocoma sumptuosa*) Andes Mountains of Ecuador and Colombia

Description 200 mm (8 in.). A large and handsome tanager from the Andes where it is found at altitudes up to 1850 m (6000 ft). Head, nape and under surfaces bright yellow; forehead, sides of head, back and rump velvety black; wings and tail black, the feathers edged with turquoise-blue; large cobalt-blue patch on shoulders. Bill black; legs grey-black. The sexes are alike.

General Management These large tanagers should be housed in a spacious outdoor aviary. They are not suitable for conservatories or greenhouses; coming from relatively high altitudes in the Andes they will not thrive in moist, humid conditions. Acclimatisation is not difficult but these birds may take a little time to adjust to a changed atmosphere. They should never be associated with smaller or weaker companions.

Breeding Mountain Tanagers are difficult birds to sex and most aviculturists will have to make a snap judgement when obtaining two birds which they hope will prove to be a pair.
Spacious, secluded accommodation with plenty of vegetation should be allocated to the birds. They will build a nest in a bush, or may be persuaded to use a wicker basket.
Insectile food, fruit, berries and plenty of small live insects should be provided if a pair succeed in hatching chicks.

Feeding This species needs a varied diet in which fruit figures prominently. Diced apples, pears, grapes and bananas, soaked currants, various berries, etc. should be offered together with a fine-grade insectivorous food. Live food should consist of cleaned maggots, mealworms and any insects from the garden. Small locusts are another valuable item for these birds.

Golden-crowned Euphonia (*Euphonia saturata*)
Northern South America

Description 115 mm (4½ in.). A small tanager with striking blue-black and yellow plumage. Mainly deep blue in colour; crown yellow; breast and under surfaces ochraceous yellow. Bill and legs black.

The female is dull green above; underparts yellow-olive with an area of yellow in the centre of the breast.

General Management Euphonias, when acclimatised, prove to be surprisingly tough. They can be housed in a planted garden aviary or a temperate conservatory. They are best provided with slight warmth during the colder months of the year, although the related Violet Euphonia (*E. violacea*) has been known to winter successfully in an unheated aviary.

Breeding These birds might be persuaded to breed in a suitable aviary. They should be supplied with wicker nest-baskets as possible nest sites.

Up to four eggs are laid and incubation is complete in 16 days. A variety of soft fruits, berries and small insects will be necessary for successful rearing of the young.

Feeding Soft fruits and berries form the bulk of their diet. They will, if given opportunity, consume nectar or sponge cake soaked in honey water to the exclusion of most other foods, but this will lead to digestive upsets and is not to be encouraged.

They should be offered a little fine-grade insectile food from time to time. Live food should also be provided; small mealworms and maggots will be accepted. Smooth caterpillars, spiders, flies, etc. should be given whenever possible.

Emerald-spotted Tanager (*Tangara guttata*)

Northern South America

Speckled Tanager

Description 130 mm (5 in.). A handsome, although not brilliantly coloured, little tanager. Delicate until acclimatised but thrives in suitable aviary or conservatory accommodation. Upper surfaces bright green; underparts mainly white; feathers of head, nape and breast spotted with black; back of head and neck suffused with golden green. Bill, upper mandible black, lower mandible light horn; legs lead-coloured.

The sexes are alike.

General Management When first obtained, these tanagers should be housed in a roomy cage or indoor flight and kept warm. Regular use of a hand-spray will maintain good plumage.

When acclimatised they can be housed in a garden aviary or conservatory. They are not sufficiently hardy to winter without heat and will be safer housed in roomy indoor quarters during the colder months. A better alternative is to keep them in a heated conservatory throughout the year. Here they will be seen at their best. Although they can prove surprisingly destructive to plant life in a small enclosure, given plenty of space they are unlikely to present too many problems in that direction.

If a greenhouse or conservatory is being specially set-up for these or similar birds it will be wise to make use of plants with large, tough leaves. Various palms, *Monstera*, *Ficus*, etc. can be inter-planted with more delicate species.

Breeding None of the *Tangara* genus can be regarded as reliable breeding prospects for the aviculturist. But most of them are sufficiently beautiful to warrant efforts being made to persuade them to go to nest. Conservatory conditions are likely to be more suitable than a garden aviary.

They build an open-cup nest. Both sexes share construction but only the female undertakes incubation. The normal clutch consists of two eggs. They hatch after about 14 days and the chicks leave the nest about three weeks later.

Plenty of small live food should be supplied when the eggs hatch. This is more easily accomplished in a conservatory where maggots pupate very quickly; another advantage of this type of housing is that flying insects are not able to escape as easily as in an aviary. Mealworms, maggots, spiders and smooth caterpillars can also be provided together with plenty of soft fruit.

Feeding Various fruits provide the bulk of the Emerald-spotted Tanager's diet. They will take pears, sweet oranges, apples and grapes. They can also have sponge cake soaked in honey water and regular supplies of live food.

Superb Tanager (*Tangara fastuosa*) Brazil
Seven-coloured Tanager

Description 140 mm (5½ in.). A vividly coloured little bird; parts of the plumage have a shimmering, metallic quality which further highlights its brilliance. Head and neck iridescent emerald-green; upper breast, back, wings and tail black, the last two edged with purple; breast and under surfaces shimmering blue, becoming more purple on the belly; lower back and rump bright orange. Bill and legs black.

The sexes are identical.

General Management Newly obtained Superb Tanagers should be housed in spacious cages in a warm, quiet room. During the winter months particular care should be paid to the process of acclimatisation and no attempt made to reduce the temperature to less than 16 °C (60 °F) until spring.

When acclimatised they live well in a garden aviary or conservatory. During the coldest months they should have a warm shelter and are best not allowed outside during periods of really severe weather.

Breeding A sheltered garden aviary or a conservatory will provide the best kind of breeding accommodation for these birds. Plenty of suitable natural cover is essential; for this reason the conservatory is perhaps a better proposition than an aviary.

Superb Tanagers may build their cup-shaped nest in a convenient bush. Alternatively, they make use of a 'starter' nest: a handful of dry grass or rootlets placed in a suitably shaped remnant of wire-netting.

So far as is known, the female incubates two eggs for a period of about 15 days. The adults' normal diet should be supplemented with items of extra live food, berries, etc. as aids to successful rearing.

Feeding A varied diet of soft fruits, live insects, a fine-grade insectile mixture, and sponge cake soaked in honey water should be provided. Fruit is best chopped into tiny cubes which the birds swallow whole. Ripe (but never overripe) pears, grapes and sweet oranges are among the best fruits to offer. Banana is popular but tends to be rather fattening and should be offered in moderation.

Raspberries, blackberries, elderberries and the like should be given when they are in season; some birds become very fond of both wild and cultivated berries, others ignore them completely.

Mealworms and maggots should be given sparingly – not more than two or three mealworms and up to half a dozen maggots. Other items of live food such as spiders, caterpillars, etc. can be given more freely.

As will be recognised, much of the food consumed by these birds is of a soft and sticky nature. If their plumage is to remain in good condition adequate bathing facilities must be provided. Careful use of a garden syringe, filled with tepid water, to spray both birds and plants will have a beneficial effect.

Indian Zosterop (*Zosterops palpebrosa*) India
Indian White-eye

Description 100 mm (4 in.). Delightful little warbler-like birds with conspicuous white eye-rings. Whole of upper surfaces bright green; chin and throat yellow; lower breast and belly grey-white, ring of feathers around eye white. Bill black; legs lead-coloured.
The sexes are alike.

General Management Zosterops are a charming addition to any collection of small foreign birds. When acclimatised they thrive in a garden aviary or alternatively in a greenhouse or conservatory. Despite their fragile appearance they are remarkably hardy and can be wintered outside provided they have access to a frost-free shelter.

Breeding Three or four eggs are laid in a small cup-shaped nest made of fine rootlets and grass. The young are fed on quantities of small insects; aphis and blackfly are valuable, together with fruit flies, spiders, etc.

Breeding pairs of Indian Zosterops can be surprisingly pugnacious and are best given a small aviary to themselves.

Feeding Indian Zosterops are particularly fond of pears. These, together with other fruits such as sweet oranges and grapes, provide the bulk of their diet. They should also be offered some fine-grade insectile food and sponge cake soaked in honey water.

Small live food is essential and Indian Zosterops should have small mealworms, maggots, spiders, flies, etc.

Chestnut-flanked Zosterop (*Zosterops mayottensis*)
Comoro Islands

Description 115 mm (4½ in.). Excellent subjects for planted aviaries or conservatory accommodation. Upper surfaces grey-green; chin and throat yellow; breast and underparts grey-white; flanks chestnut; eye-rings white. Bill black; legs grey.
The sexes are alike.

General Management These little birds become quite hardy and can remain outside throughout the year provided a comfortable shelter is provided for them. They are at home in a planted garden aviary or a temperate conservatory.

Breeding Provided a true pair is available there is no reason why breeding should not be accomplished. They are unlikely to nest if they have to compete with other birds in the same aviary, and a small, secluded flight should be provided for their sole occupation if possible. An abundant supply of small insects – aphis, blackfly, fruit flies, etc. – is essential for successful rearing of young.

Feeding Fruit, including sweet oranges, pears and grapes, forms the greater part of a staple diet. They should also have some sponge cake soaked in honey water. Live food should be given each day. They should also be given regular supplies of a fine-grade insectile mixture. They are adept at capturing small flies and if housed in a greenhouse or conservatory efforts should be made to establish a culture of fruit flies for them.

Van Hasselt's Sunbird (*Cinnyris sperata*) South-east Asia

Description 100 mm (4 in.). One of the smallest and most beautiful of the Asiatic sunbirds. Infrequently available, but lives well in a conservatory or planted garden aviary. Upper parts black with metallic purple-blue gloss; forehead to nape iridescent gold-green; chin and throat metallic amethyst; breast deep maroon merging into black on the lower under surfaces. Bill and legs black.

Females are mainly olive-green above with yellow underparts.

General Management Like most of the sunbirds, this species needs careful handling when first obtained and should be acquired only by experienced aviculturists. Newly imported birds must be housed in roomy flights in a warm birdroom.

Once acclimatised they can be moved to more temperate accommodation. They do well in sheltered garden aviaries and are excellent occupants for a conservatory. They can be housed with other small nectar-feeding species but a breeding pair should be housed alone.

A garden aviary to accommodate these little birds should have part of the flight covered with polythene or some similar type of glass substitute to provide shelter from cold winds and driving rain. Plenty of vegetation should be provided, including climbing plants, among which the birds will capture small insects.

Although they become quite hardy, Van Hasselt's Sunbirds are best not exposed to extremely low temperatures and should be either shut into a comfortable shelter during the winter months or housed in roomy cages in the birdroom.

A planted conservatory probably represents ideal accommodation for these little birds and there is perhaps a greater prospect of breeding from them among the lush vegetation which can be propagated in this type of environment.

Breeding Sunbirds are among the most difficult of small exotic species to breed in controlled conditions. They are unlikely to succeed unless provided with suitable accommodation which they do not have to share with other species.

They are unlikely to make use of any artificial nesting receptacles but should be given a variety of suitable materials from which to construct their own nest; fine grasses, moss, etc. would be suitable.

Ample supplies of small live food are necessary when young are being reared. In a greenhouse or conservatory, fruit flies can be bred in sufficient quantity; alternatively, greenfly, blackfly and similar small insects must be used.

Feeding One of the proprietary artificial nectar mixtures will suit these birds. They must also have some live food; some birds will attempt to eat small maggots and mealworms but they are much more likely to remain in good health if provided with regular supplies of small flying insects.

Verditer Flycatcher (*Stoparola melanops*)
Himalayas eastwards to Burma and western China

Description 150 mm (6 in.). Attractively coloured birds which become tame and confiding. At their best in a planted garden aviary. Small patch at base of bill black; wings and tail showing some brown; remainder of plumage blue-green. Bill and legs black.

The female is similar but colours are much more dull. Some white flecks on chin and throat.

General Management Like most small insectivorous species, Verditer Flycatchers need considerable care when first obtained. They frequently prove difficult to wean on to substitute foods.

Once established, however, they make excellent occupants for a garden aviary and usually prove surprisingly hardy. They should be provided with a comfortable shelter for use during severe weather, but acclimatised specimens will frequently choose to roost outside throughout the year and appear to suffer no harm as a result.

They are great bathers and should be given every opportunity for a daily dip. Freshly acquired specimens may need to be sprayed with tepid water until they have settled down.

Breeding While male Verditer Flycatchers are often obtainable, females are more difficult to acquire. A true pair should be provided with a small planted aviary of which they are the sole occupants.

The birds may make use of an open wicker basket but it is more likely they will construct their own cup-shaped nest. While a shrub or bush might be chosen as a suitable site, this species is more likely to be attracted by an ivy-clad wall or a bank against which other creeping or climbing plants provide cover.

Usually four eggs are laid and incubation is complete in about a fortnight. It is from this point on that the aviculturist's problems begin in earnest for the brood will not be reared unless a continuous supply of small live food can be supplied – at least until they are fledged. Small mealworms and housefly maggots will be taken but it is essential that other items such as ant pupae, small smooth caterpillars, flying insects, etc. are also supplied.

Feeding A good quality, fine-grade insectile mixture provides a staple diet for these birds. They must also have a variety of live food. Maggots can be allowed to complete their life-cycle to emerge as blowflies. Kept in a tube or container with a small aperture through which they can emerge when hatched, they provide a valuable item of diet for birds of this kind.

Rufous-bellied Niltava (*Niltava sundara*)
Himalayas eastwards to Burma and China

Description 150 mm (6 in.). One of the most beautiful of the small Asiatic flycatchers and a highly desirable aviary bird. Forehead, sides of head and throat velvety black; crown, sides of neck, shoulders and rump iridescent cobalt-blue; remainder of upper surfaces dark blue; breast and underparts bright chestnut; wings dark brown edged with blue; tail black edged with blue. Bill black; legs dark brown.

Females are mainly olive-brown with paler under surfaces; throat whitish; tail chestnut; shining blue patch on each side of neck.

General Management While not markedly delicate, these birds can be difficult to acclimatise and are best acquired only by experienced aviculturists. Once established they thrive in outdoor aviaries and are remarkably hardy.

They should be housed in a planted aviary with access to a shelter. Heat is not required, even in winter, once the birds are properly acclimatised. Niltavas often choose to roost in the most exposed parts of their aviary amid snow and frost – and come to no harm as a result.

Breeding While niltavas have been bred on a number of occasions, the occurrence is still, unfortunately, a rare one. If a true pair can be obtained it is worth persevering even if success is not achieved at first.

The breeding aviary should have abundant cover. Provide one or two artificial nesting sites such as boxes or wicker baskets. Niltavas build a cup-shaped nest, usually fairly low down and concealed in a thicket of vegetation. The clutch usually consists of four eggs. Incubation lasts for 13 days.

These highly insectivorous little birds need an abundant supply of live food if they are to rear their brood successfully. Live ant pupae, wasp grubs, smooth caterpillars, spiders, blowflies, fruit flies and aphis should all find their place on the menu at this time. A piece of rotting meat or fish can be suspended in the flight to attract more flies.

Feeding Although freshly obtained niltavas are often difficult to accustom to substitute foods, once the transition has been made they rarely look back. They should have a fine-grade insectile mixture to which should be added (two or three times a week) some very finely scraped raw meat, grated dry cheese, grated carrot and apple.

Live food is essential. Small mealworms and maggots should be offered in moderation. Efforts should be made to vary this natural part of the birds' menu with items collected in the garden – spiders, small moths, blowflies and other flying insects are excellent. Even the humble woodlouse provides welcome variety.

Yellow-collared Ixulus (Ixulus flavicollis) Himalayas

Description 100 mm (4½ in.). Small and rather soberly coloured little birds. Attractive in a planted conservatory. Upper surfaces olive-brown; nape yellowish; underparts grey-white; crest dark brown. Bill and legs brown.

The sexes are alike.

General Management These interesting little birds are kept in aviaries rather infrequently. They are active and acrobatic in habit.

Newly obtained ixulus require careful handling. They should be housed in a spacious cage and kept warm for the first few weeks. Their temporary quarters should be furnished with one or two twiggy branches which will need to be renewed at frequent intervals as they become sticky; after feeding, the birds wipe the sticky residue from their bills on to a convenient perch and their plumage will suffer if the branches are not replaced regularly.

Ixulus can be housed in a small aviary during the warm summer months. They can be allowed outside during periods of cold weather provided they have the opportunity to return to a comfortable shelter at all times. Alternatively they do well in a planted greenhouse or conservatory.

Breeding Not a great deal is known about the species' breeding habits. Although at most times they are quiet and somewhat inoffensive little birds, if they decide to nest their attitude changes considerably and they are quite capable of putting birds twice their size to flight.

Plenty of cover should be provided in their aviary with the objective of producing a variety of suitable nest sites in the most secluded parts of the flight.

They would be unlikely to rear young without abundant supplies of small insects; fruit flies can be produced in a conservatory setting. Other useful items would include greenfly, blackfly, spiders, houseflies, etc.

Feeding Given the opportunity, ixulus will feed almost exclusively on a nectar mixture of honey and water but it is important they take a more varied diet. While nectar should be included in their diet the quantity must be carefully regulated.

They enjoy soft fruits such as pears and grapes; berries can be offered as they come into season. Provide a fine-grade insectile mixture, some sponge cake soaked in honey water and small insects. Mealworms and maggots may prove too tough for these tiny birds and fruit flies provide a better alternative. They will also take houseflies and blowflies.

Black-Chinned Yuhina (*Yuhina nigrimentum*) Himalayas

Description 100 mm (4 in.). Very attractive despite their lack of bright colours. Upper surfaces dark olive-brown; underparts greyish white, tinged with buff on the abdomen; crest and chin black. Bill brown, orange at base; legs red-brown.

The sexes are alike.

General Management Yuhinas need careful acclimatisation, but can then be housed in a planted garden aviary or conservatory. They should have a dry and frost-free shelter for use during the winter months. Once acclimatised they do not mind low temperatures, but will not survive outside without some protection from chill damp winters.

Despite their small size, males are extremely aggressive in defence of territory and quite capable of putting birds more than twice their size to flight.

Breeding Yuhinas are unlikely to attempt to breed unless they are the sole occupants of a small aviary or conservatory. They prefer to build their nest in a shrub or climbing plant and should be provided with plenty of fine grass and rootlets for this purpose.

Plenty of small live insects will be required for rearing purposes. Fruit flies, aphis, blackfly, houseflies and the like should be supplied in quantity.

Feeding Various fruits – pears, grapes and sweet oranges – provide the mainstay of the yuhinas' diet. They also enjoy sponge cake soaked in honey water. Berries are taken. Small live insects should be given; mealworms and maggots seem to be too tough-skinned for these tiny birds, and other, more palatable intems should be gathered from the garden whenever possible. Some fine-grade insectile food should always be available.

110

Pekin Robin (*Leiothrix lutea*)
Himalayas and southern China
Red-billed Leiothrix, Pekin Nightingale

Description 150 mm (6 in.). A delightful little babbler which has good looks and a fine song. Upper surfaces olive-green; throat yellow, merging into an orange breast; lower breast greyish yellow; webs of wing feathers edged with orange and red. Bill red; legs pinkish. Females are similar but the yellow and orange of the throat and upper breast are paler.

General Management In most respects Pekin Robins are the ideal beginner's softbill. They flourish in outdoor aviaries and with proper care will live for many years. They become hardy enough to winter without heat.

They are rarely still and if not flitting about the vegetation they will probably be bathing. They are fastidious about their appearance and take several baths each day.

The males have a pretty flute-like song heard throughout the year, except during the moult.

Breeding A breeding pair of Pekin Robins should have an aviary to themselves. Some construct their nest – a deep cup-shaped affair – in a bush; others prefer a box or basket.

Incubation of the three or four eggs is carried out by both sexes. The eggs hatch after 14 days. Plenty of extra live food should be supplied when young are being reared.

Feeding Pekin Robins are omnivorous and will accept a wide variety of foods. Ideally they should have a coarse-grade insectile mixture, various fruits and live food. Cleaned maggots and an occasional mealworm will suffice in this latter direction. From time to time the diet can be varied with seeds, berries, green food – and even vegetables.

Black-headed Sibia (*Leioptila capistrata*) Himalayas

Description 250 mm (10 in.). Active, rather jay-like birds which thrive in suitable aviaries. They become very hardy. Upper and lower surfaces rufous-brown; back and wings grey-brown; head, including an erectile crest, black; tail red-brown banded with black and slate-grey at tip. Bill black; legs red-brown.

The sexes are alike.

General Management Because of their size and active disposition these are essentially birds for a spacious aviary. After a period of acclimatisation they become extremely hardy and can winter outside provided they have access to a frost-free shelter.

They are almost constantly on the move and need plenty of space. Their flight is best furnished with suitable shrubs and bushes.

Breeding If a true pair can be obtained they should be housed alone in a suitable aviary. They build a cup-shaped nest, fairly high up. They may be persuaded to make use of an old nest as a foundation.

The young are fed on live food and fruit, mainly the former. Maggots, mealworms, grass-hoppers, locusts and beetles should be supplied when young are being reared.

Feeding Sibias are easy to feed. Their staple diet consists of a good-quality insectivorous mixture, fruit of all kinds and a daily allowance of live food. They also appreciate some finely chopped raw meat from time to time.

White-crested Jay-Thrush (*Garrulax leucolophus*) India
White-crested Laughing Thrush

Description 300 mm (12 in.). Handsome and amusing birds which need plenty of space and should not be housed with smaller or weaker companions. Back, wings and tail dark chocolate-brown; head – including crest – and breast white; mask from base of bill to cheeks black; under surfaces brown. Bill black; legs dark grey.
The sexes are alike.

General Management Active and inquisitive, these handsome birds are extremely playful and a pair will indulge in all manner of amusing antics. They are very noisy and may upset neighbours who do not share an enthusiasm for bird-keeping!
When acclimatised they can be wintered outside. A shelter should be provided but jay-thrushes are tough customers and they may prefer to roost outside throughout the year.

Breeding These are by no means the easiest of birds to breed from in aviaries. A spacious, secluded flight with plenty of natural cover will provide the best chance of success.
Plenty of live food is required if chicks are to be reared successfully. Locusts are excellent; baby mice, frogs and newts also figure in the diet at this time.

Feeding Jay-thrushes need a varied diet if they are to remain in good health. A coarse-grade insectivorous mixture provides the basis; minced raw meat should be added two or three times a week. Provide them with plenty of live food – mealworms, maggots, locusts and grasshoppers. They are also fond of fruit.

Shama (*Copsychus malabaricus*) India

Description 280 mm (11 in.) including a graduated tail of 150 mm (6 in.). An extremely popular Asiatic softbill, generally recognised as one of the world's great feathered songsters. Head, back and breast glossy black; lower breast and underparts rich chestnut; rump white; tail black with white outer feathers. Bill black; legs flesh-coloured.

Females have dull-brown upper surfaces and breast; the feathers of the lower breast are rufous. The female's tail is also shorter.

General Management Shamas are among the most attractive aviary birds. Intelligent and friendly, they adapt quickly to aviary life, are easily fed and become reasonably hardy.

When acclimatised – and the species needs care and gentle handling until this is accomplished – shamas will live in a garden aviary. A pair should be housed alone; males can be particularly aggressive during the breeding season and are capable of killing birds twice their size.

Breeding Shamas will make use of a box or basket, or even an old nest, as a foundation for their own. Four or five eggs are laid. The male usually helps to build the nest; he takes no part in incubation duties but whiles away the time singing.

Sometimes an over-enthusiastic male will chase and upset his mate while incubation and rearing are taking place. Individual birds vary a great deal in this respect; some males have to be banished from the breeding aviary, others prove to be model fathers and assist in feeding their offspring.

A wide assortment of live food is essential when chicks are being reared. If the aviculturist can obtain such items as ant pupae, smooth caterpillars, spiders, woodlice, small grasshoppers, blowflies and so on in sufficient quantity all will be well. Some people, however, prefer to release the adult birds to forage in the garden while they have unfledged young to feed. Needless to say, the parents must be confined again just before the chicks leave the nest and become self-supporting.

Feeding Shamas should be given a fine-grade insectile mixture as basic diet. To this one can add small quantities of grated cheese, hard-boiled egg yolk and some scraped lean raw meat.

A variety of live insects is essential. Although mealworms and cleaned maggots can provide the bulk – especially during the winter months when little else is available – every effort should be made to provide variety by the addition of an occasional spider, small locusts and the like.

Some aviculturists offer fruit and green food. Few shamas show interest in these items. Some finely shredded greenstuff can be mixed with their soft food from time to time.

Common Rubythroat (*Luscinia calliope*) Northern Asia
Siberian Rubythroat

Description 140 mm (5½ in.). A soberly coloured little bird but with distinctive throat markings which give it its popular name. Upper surfaces, wings and tail uniform olive-brown; underparts grey-brown shading to whitish on abdomen; chin and throat ruby-scarlet with narrow black border; small area of black in front of eye; white eyebrow and moustachial streaks. Bill black; legs dark horn.

Females have less clearly defined markings and lack the distinctive throat patterning.

General Management Aggressive little birds, and not to be trusted in mixed company. Once established they thrive in a garden aviary. The flight should have plenty of growing plants, including some thickets of evergreen, for these birds invariably choose to roost outside.

Breeding Both birds must be in peak breeding condition; if the female's enthusiasm does not quite match that of her mate she will almost certainly be subjected to savage persecution. The birds will sometimes build a nest in the depths of a thicket; alternatively they may use a cup-shaped wicker basket.

Plenty of small live food is required if chicks are to be reared successfully. Live ant pupae, wasp grubs, smooth green caterpillars, grasshoppers and the like can be collected, although the work is hard and painstaking.

Feeding A fine-grade insectile mixture provides the basic diet for these birds. Dried grated cheese, scraped raw beef and hard-boiled egg yolk can be added from time to time. Small live food is all important and every effort should be made to provide as wide a variety of insects as possible.

Coppersmith Barbet (*Megalaima haemacephala*)
India and Ceylon eastwards to Malaysia, Sumatra and the Philippines
Crimson-breasted Barbet

Description 150 mm (6 in.). One of the smaller Asiatic barbets. Named because of its unusual call-note which resembles a small hammer striking metal. Forehead, crown and a broad band across the breast crimson; chin, throat and small patches above and below the eye bright yellow; top of head and cheeks dull black; upper surfaces grass-green; remainder of underparts pale greyish white patterned with streaks of dark green. Bill black; legs red. The sexes are alike.

General Management These are difficult birds to establish and should not be acquired by the inexperienced aviculturist.

They are best caged in a warm room to begin with. They should be provided with a box in which to sleep. It is essential their quarters are maintained in a scrupulously clean condition and the birds should be sprayed regularly with tepid water to maintain their plumage in a clean condition.

Breeding This species provides a real challenge for the aviculturist intent on breeding success. They are likely to nest only in ideal planted aviary conditions and should be provided with boxes or hollow logs. Plenty of soft fruits and some live food would be required to feed any resulting youngsters.

Feeding Coppersmith Barbets feed almost exclusively on soft fruits. They should have diced pear, apple and grape. Some fine-grade insectile mixture should be provided together with a daily ration of live food.

117

Cedar Waxwing (*Bombycilla cedrorum*) North America

Description 150 mm (6 in.). Handsome birds with beautiful silk-smooth plumage. Head, back and upper breast soft pinkish olive; lower breast grey-brown; rump and tail grey – tail tipped with yellow; broad black stripe from base of bill, through eye to crown; small white moustachial stripe; flight feathers black; secondaries with sealing-wax red appendages. The species has a distinctive crest. Bill and legs black.

The sexes are alike.

General Management Easily managed birds which soon become tame and confiding. Unfortunately they tend to be somewhat lethargic and will become fat and unhealthy unless housed in reasonably large aviaries and given a carefully controlled diet.

A garden aviary to house these birds should offer ample flying space. It is a good plan to site food and water vessels well away from favourite perches so that flying exercise is necessary to reach them.

They are gregarious by nature and a group may live amicably in spacious quarters.

Breeding Waxwings have proved somewhat unwilling breeders under controlled conditions, but it is possible that several pairs sharing the same aviary would be more likely to settle down to nesting than an isolated couple.

Plenty of natural cover should be provided in the breeding aviary. Fairly tall-growing *Cupressus* and other evergreens might fit the requirement. One or two cup-shaped wicker baskets and open-topped boxes should be fixed securely in place – fairly high and in the more dense patches of vegetation.

A successful hatching of young waxwings may mark the start of problems for their owner. For while the adults feed almost exclusively on berries throughout most of the year they switch to insects during the breeding season – mainly flies, gnats and mosquitoes.

To achieve complete success it may be necessary to supply a captive breeding pair with large quantities of fruit flies, houseflies and blowflies.

Feeding Cedar Waxwings should be given a varied diet which includes insectile food, soaked currants and sultanas, various berries and some finely chopped apple. The birds invariably opt for berries. It is essential that supplies of high-protein items such as currants and sultanas are limited.

Much valuable food can be gathered during the autumn. Mountain ash berries are a great favourite; others which can be tried include elderberries, cotoneaster and pyracanthus berries.

Except during the breeding season live food seems not to interest these birds a great deal.

Golden-fronted Fruitsucker (*Chloropsis aurifrons*)

Northern India, Burma
Golden-fronted Leafbird, Golden-fronted Chloropsis

Description 200 mm (8 in.). Popular Asiatic softbills which live well in aviaries. Mainly bright green in colour; throat cobalt-blue, black edged with yellow; moustachial streak; front of head golden orange; shoulder patch turquoise-blue. Bill black; legs dark grey. The sexes are similar.

General Management Newly acquired birds should be kept warm and, even during the summer months, no attempt should be made to house them outside until they are properly acclimatised. They are best housed in roomy flight cages for the first few weeks. Give them facilities for frequent bathing and see that perches and equipment are maintained in a scrupulously clean condition.

Acclimatised birds can be housed in a planted garden aviary. They are extremely pugnacious and cannot normally be housed with other species. Although they become hardy they are probably best housed indoors during periods of severe weather and are happier in a slightly warmed room during the winter months.

Breeding A spacious planted aviary offers the best kind of accommodation for breeding these lovely birds, but even in an ideal situation it is a task not easily accomplished.

Fruitsuckers build a cup-shaped nest fairly high in the branches of a tree or shrub. They are unlikely to tolerate any disturbance should nesting occur in the aviary and must be left very much to themselves.

The young are reared on a variety of foods. Soft fruits, insects and sponge cake soaked in honey water should be provided.

Feeding Various soft fruits form the mainstay of their diet. They enjoy grapes, pears and oranges; berries should also be offered. Some examples will take a little insectile food. Sponge cake soaked in honey water or one of the proprietary nectar mixtures should be given each day. A ration of live food is also essential. Mealworms, maggots, caterpillars, blowflies, etc. should be provided daily.

Red-vented Bulbul (*Pycnonotus cafer*) India and Ceylon

Description 200 mm (8 in.). Hardy and easily managed, the Red-vented Bulbul is an excellent beginner's softbill. Head, including crest, and throat black; upper surfaces and breast dark brown, the feathers edged with white to give a scale-like effect; abdomen and upper tail coverts white with an area of bright red feathers on the vent. Bill and legs black. The sexes are alike.

General Management Although not brightly coloured this is an attractive aviary bird; cheerful and confident, it quickly becomes tame enough to feed from its owner's hand.

When acclimatised they quickly become hardy and are happy in unheated quarters throughout the year. A breeding pair need an aviary to themselves but single birds can share accommodation with other species of comparable size and temperament; Glossy starlings, mynahs, Pekin Robins and some of the larger weavers and whydahs are usually safe companions for them.

While they have no song worth speaking of, their call note is completely in character – loud and cheerful. They like to find a high vantage point in the aviary from which they will call at frequent intervals.

Breeding Given suitable accommodation in a planted aviary, a pair of Red-vented Bulbuls can usually be persuaded to nest and rear young. Their rather untidy, cup-shaped nest is usually built in a bush, against plants climbing up the sides of the aviary – or even on a shelf in the shelter. They often make use of a box or basket.

Two or three eggs are laid and both parents share nest-building, incubation and rearing. The eggs hatch in a little over two weeks and the young birds leave the nest about a fortnight later.

Plenty of live food should be supplied when the parents have young to rear. Mealworms, maggots, grasshoppers, small locusts, woodlice and smooth caterpillars are ideal.

A pair may produce two or more broods in the course of a season. It is wiser to remove their offspring as soon as they are seen to be capable of fending for themselves – otherwise they may outstay their welcome in the breeding aviary and suffer serious injury through being attacked by their parents.

Feeding A coarse-grade insectile mixture together with fruit and some live food is all that is required to keep these birds in good condition. They particularly enjoy pears and chopped grapes but will take most kinds of fruit. Berries should be offered as they become available. They need a regular daily allowance of live food. Up to six mealworms can be supplied each day. Other items can be collected from the garden to provide variety.

Bulbuls Common residents around villages and homesteads throughout southern Asia and Africa. Many have pleasant little songs, whereas others are noisy with constant musical chatterings. It is perhaps their industrious inquisitive and friendly nature that makes them attractive for the aviary. There are some 119 species making up this large family. They vary in size from 150 mm (6 in.) to 275 mm (11 in.). Males and females are generally alike, the males being slightly larger. Their outstanding characteristic is the patch of veinless, hair-like feathers on the nape.

Pileated Jay (*Cyanocorax affinis*) South America

Description 355 mm (14 in.). These handsome South American members of the crow family are excellent aviary subjects. They need plenty of space and should be housed only with birds of comparable size and temperament. Head, throat and upper breast black; nape blue-white; rest of upper surfaces blue-brown; underparts white; moustachial streak cobalt-blue. Bill black; legs grey.

The sexes are alike.

General Management These active birds are best housed in roomy outdoor aviaries. When first received they need care until acclimatised; eventually they prove to be very hardy and can be wintered outside without the need for heated quarters.

Typical of the family, they are intelligent and inquisitive. They are not safe companions for smaller birds but can usually be housed with other large softbills, doves, pheasants, etc. They should never be kept in the same aviary as other breeding stock for they will lose no opportunity of stealing either eggs or nestlings. If one has a known pair of Pileated Jays it will, in any event, prove sensible to house them alone.

Their aviary should be furnished with plenty of strongly growing shrubs and bushes. They should have a dry and frost-free shed for roosting purposes.

They have a habit of hiding odd scraps of food and it may be wise, especially during warm weather, to seek out their 'larder' and dispose of the contents from time to time.

Breeding Like most jays these birds seem to combine intelligence with extreme wariness and they are usually unwilling to nest unless provided with plenty of space and seclusion.

Their nest is a bulky structure and may be built in a bush or the birds may make use of an open-fronted box. Three to five eggs are laid and incubation is believed to take about three weeks.

Many crows and magpies, after successfully incubating a clutch of eggs, immediately dash all hopes of a successful breeding by making a meal of their own young. It is difficult to know how to combat this unfortunate tendency; probably the provision of a suitably varied natural diet at this time would help. Locusts, grasshoppers and small baby mice should be offered.

Feeding A coarse-grade insectile food can be used as a basic diet for these birds. It is essential, though, that they are given occasional mice and dead sparrows. Some minced beef can be added to the insectile food from time to time. They will also enjoy fruit and some of the more easily obtained items of live food such as mealworms and maggots.

Banded Pitta (*Pitta guajana*) Malaysia

Van den Bock's Pitta

Description 200 mm (8 in.). A handsomely marked and very beautiful ground-loving bird. Head black, with a prominent eyebrow stripe shading from golden yellow to orange; upper surfaces brown; chin and throat white; patch on sides of neck yellow; under surfaces blue; sides of breast with alternating bands of orange and blue; tail dark blue. Bill black; legs grey. The female is a much more soberly coloured bird, lacking her mate's brilliant colours but showing some barring on the sides of the breast.

General Management While they usually appear in good condition pittas can quickly come to grief in inexperienced hands. They are frequently unwilling to accept substitute foods and great patience may be required before they will accept a change.

But the biggest source of failure with these lovely birds lies in the provision of an unsuitable environment. It is vital that they are provided with a thick, springy carpet of peat, dead leaves, etc. and that this is maintained in a moist condition at all times. They need roomy flights to begin with and the floor should be carpeted to a depth of about 100 mm (4 in.) with a suitable mixture of leaves, peat, etc. One or two rotten branches and a stone will suffice as perches – one of which should be fixed as high as possible since pittas like to roost well off the ground.

They are best housed in conservatories. Alternatively they do well in suitable outdoor aviaries during the summer months but need some warmth during the colder part of the year.

Breeding Pittas have been bred infrequently. One of the major difficulties appears to be in achieving a degree of tolerance between the breeding pair; both must be in breeding condition before being allowed to share the same enclosure.

A greenhouse or conservatory probably provides the best type of accommodation for a potential breeding pair of these birds. Not a great deal is known about their breeding habits, apart from the fact that they build a rather bulky nest – rather like a football in size and shape – at or a little above ground level.

Feeding A good-quality fine-grade insectile food suits these birds. Minced raw beef should be added two or three times a week, together with the yolk of a hard-boiled egg. Live food is essential and pittas will take mealworms, maggots, small locusts, grasshoppers, beetles and snails. Some of the larger species enjoy an occasional small mouse or bird.

Spot-billed Toucanet (*Selenidera maculirostris*)

Southern Brazil westwards to north-eastern Argentina

Description 250 mm (10 in.). One of the smaller and more easily housed members of the toucan family. Despite a somewhat malevolent appearance they are attractive and interesting birds. Head, nape and under surfaces black; upper parts dark green; cheeks orange; area of blue from base of bill to cheeks, under tail coverts red. Bill pale green-blue with black markings; legs grey.

The female's plumage is more muted; the black areas are replaced by feathers of dark brown, while the area of bare skin extending from the base of the bill is of a more greenish hue.

General Management These small toucans, when acclimatised, can be housed in either conservatories or garden aviaries. Unfortunately they usually create havoc with most forms of plant life and if vegetation is to be included in their quarters it is best planted in pots or tubs so that some sort of rotation system can be employed before the toucanets achieve total destruction.

In no circumstances should they be kept outside until they are fully acclimatised.

They do well in outdoor aviaries but are not hardy enough to remain outside during the winter months unless provided with a warm shelter.

Individual birds vary in their willingness to live with other species but they are generally fairly peaceful and can be housed with some of the larger softbills such as Glossy Starlings, jay-thrushes, etc.

Breeding This species, like other toucans, must be regarded as a difficult breeding prospect for the aviculturist. A pair should be housed in a spacious aviary and supplied with a variety of nest-boxes and hollow logs. Bunches of spruce can be employed to provide a reasonably natural-looking site.

The three or four eggs hatch after an incubation period of about 16 days and the chicks remain in the nest for a further five to six weeks.

Apart from additional supplies of fruit and live foods it is unlikely the adults will require any extra foods to rear their brood.

Feeding Various fruits – apples, pears, grapes, etc. – chopped into small cubes should be offered. Toucanets should also have some insectivorous food; this can be given either sprinkled on the fruit or formed into small, soft balls containing a mixture of fruit, insectile food and a small amount of raw meat.

Mealworms, small locusts, grasshoppers and other items of live food should be offered regularly.

Toco Toucan (*Ramphastos toco*)

Guianas, Brazil, Paraguay, northern Argentina and Bolivia

Description 500 mm (20 in.). Delightful birds, particularly if they have been hand-reared. Usually very tame and confiding. Cheeks, throat, breast and rump white; white area on breast edged with yellow; under tail coverts red; remainder of plumage velvety black. Bill 200 mm (8 in.) yellow-orange with broad black band at base of upper and lower mandibles and large area of black at tip of upper mandible. Legs blue-grey.

The sexes are alike.

General Management It is the lot of many toucans purchased by amateur aviculturists to be kept as 'pets', usually in totally unsuitable accommodation. Despite their quaint appearance and friendly disposition it is strongly recommended that they are purchased only by people who have suitable aviaries or tropical-house-type accommodation for them.

When acclimatised they eventually become quite hardy and can be allowed outside even during the winter months provided they have comfortable sleeping quarters. Damp conditions, fog and cold winds can cause chills and care should be exercised in allowing them outside during severe weather.

They need plenty of space and their quarters should be as lofty as possible; toucans spend little time at ground level and prefer to leap among high perches.

A temperate conservatory or large greenhouse can also be used to house these birds. Unfortunately they are not safe companions for smaller species. They are also destructive to plant life and there is little point in furnishing their quarters with expensive vegetation.

Breeding Here is a challenge to tax the patience and ingenuity of even the most experienced aviculturist! Provided a true pair is available and given suitable accommodation there seems no reason why they should not be persuaded to breed.

A pair should be provided with either hollow logs or suitably disguised nest-boxes fixed into place in the highest parts of the aviary.

It is likely that a good deal of animal food would be needed to supplement the birds' normal diet if young were hatched – mice, frogs, newts, locusts and even small birds could be offered.

Feeding Toucans require a varied diet. While fruit forms the bulk of their intake it is essential they are given an insectivorous mixture and some raw meat. It may be necessary to make up pellets containing fruit, meat and insectile food if the birds refuse to take the last two items. Apple, pears, grapes, etc. should be offered diced into small cubes. Soaked raisins and sultanas can be given. Most toucans enjoy an occasional small dead mouse.

Sparkling Violet-eared Humming Bird (*Colibri coruscans*)
Colombia and Venezuela to northern Argentina

Description 140 mm (5½ in.). One of the best-known and most widely kept members of this large family. Mainly iridescent green in colour; chin, throat ear patches and centre of belly glittering purplish blue. Bill and legs black.

The sexes are alike.

General Management Despite the advances which have been made within recent years in the care and management of most nectar-feeding species, humming birds should not be acquired by the inexperienced aviculturist. They are *not* easy to maintain in good health over long periods and it calls for a good deal of skill and experience to achieve long-term success with them.

Newly acquired birds can be housed at first in roomy cages or indoor flights. They are at their best in a suitable conservatory or greenhouse; during the summer months many species (including the Sparkling Violet-ear) thrive in planted garden aviaries.

When they are housed temporarily in cages, it is usual to provide only one or two very thin perches. The feeding tube must be fixed in such a way that the bird can feed on the wing without fear of damaging flight feathers while hovering. Since it is unlikely caged hummers will bathe, frequent use of a small hand-spray is called for.

When acclimatised, many species of humming birds prove to be remarkably hardy. They are more likely to succumb in overheated conditions than when housed at moderate temperatures.

Breeding Various humming birds have bred successfully in controlled conditions. Pairs should have accommodation of their own; they are extremely aggressive little birds and a pair intent on breeding is unlikely to tolerate companions.

The tiny, cup-shaped nest is usually built in the fork of some slender branches. Two eggs are laid. While male humming birds do not normally play any part in incubation the Sparkling Violet-ear is a rare exception.

An abundant supply of small flying insects must be provided if chicks are hatched out. It is probable that houseflies would be taken in addition to Drosophila (fruit flies).

Feeding There are many schools of thought regarding the most suitable diet for humming birds. One of the proprietary nectar mixtures is the most popular staple diet, although some aviculturists have their own particular mixtures. Whatever type of nectar is selected it is important that the liquid diet is supplemented with plenty of fruit flies. Water should always be available, both for drinking purposes and bathing.

It is imperative that feeders should be kept scrupulously clean.

Artificial Nectar for Humming Birds The following is a widely used and proven diet for humming birds. Dissolve 110 g (4 oz) of cane sugar in 0·25 litre (½ pint) of boiling water; allow to cool. Mix a level teaspoonful of Gevral-Protein with *cold* water to form a smooth paste. This should be added to the sugar water only when the latter is cold. Stir well before use.

Bourke's Parrakeet (*Neophema bourkii*)

Central Australia

Description 230 mm (9 in.). A delightful little bird, quietly coloured but with a particularly beautiful pastel-shaded plumage. Widely kept and easily bred. Upper surfaces grey-brown; forehead pale blue; breast and underparts pink-brown; some violet-blue in wings and tail. Bill dark horn; legs grey-brown.

The female is usually slightly smaller and shows little or no blue on the forehead.

General Management With the exception of the cockatiel and budgerigar this is probably the best-known and most widely kept of all Australian parrakeets. The parrakeets are very easy to manage and are one of the few parrot-like birds which can be housed with reasonable safety in a planted aviary. Bourke's Parrakeets can be housed with small finches and soft-bills, and will even breed in a mixed aviary although, like most birds, they usually produce better results if given an aviary to themselves.

These attractive birds do not require a large aviary. They are hardy and can be wintered outside without heat although they should be provided with a dry and frost-free shelter.

Bourke's Parrakeets have been bred in cages but this is a practice with little to recommend it; the resulting progeny will almost certainly prove to be lacking in vigour and of generally inferior quality.

Breeding Given a suitable aviary, Bourke's Parrakeets usually breed freely. They will make use of either boxes or hollow logs – the former are quite acceptable and probably more convenient and easily obtained.

Three to six eggs are laid and incubation lasts about 18 days. Wood shavings or a piece of turf with a saucer-shaped depression cut into it should be placed in the base of the nest-box. They will rear their youngsters without addition to their normal diet but should have extra greenstuff, seeding grasses, etc. during the breeding season.

Feeding A staple diet for these birds should include plain canary seed, white and yellow millets, hulled oats and groats. Small quantities of hemp and sunflower seed should be added from time to time.

Spray millet, seeding grass heads, unripened heads of wheat and oats should also be offered whenever available. Bourke's Parrakeets are also fond of greenstuff and will enjoy chickweed, dandelion, groundsel and so on. Grit and cuttlefish bone should always be available.

Turquoisine Grass Parrakeet (*Neophema pulchella*)

South-eastern Australia

Turquoise Parrakeet

Description 190 mm (7½ in.). One of the most beautiful of the grass parrakeets. Established pairs usually breed freely. Upper surfaces mainly grass-green; underparts yellow; forehead, top of head, chin and throat bright turquoise-blue; shoulder patch red; wings and tail showing various shades of blue, green and yellow. Bill grey-black; legs grey.

Females are less brightly coloured; they lack the red wing patches and the blue of the face and cheeks is paler.

General Management These beautiful little parrakeets are seen at their best in a spacious flight. Provided a comfortable, dry shelter is available they do not require heat during the winter months.

Turquoisines are among the most popular and widely kept of the grass parrakeets. They are not difficult to manage and have much to recommend them as a species suitable for relatively inexperienced aviculturists.

An aviary to house a pair of turquoisines should be as large as possible. Their flight, although swift, is a little less direct than that of related species; towards dusk they tend to become quite active and swoop about like multicoloured bats in the half-light.

Breeding Suitable nest-boxes are best hung in a sheltered part of the flight. Some decayed wood should be placed in the bottom. The four or five eggs are incubated for about 20 days by the female. They leave the nest about four weeks later.

The male is usually extremely attentive while his mate is incubating, although on occasions some birds appear to grow tired of their matrimonial duties and will attempt to persuade their mates (sometimes by force!) to abandon their brood. In these circumstances the only thing one can do is remove the offending male bird and hope that his mate will succeed in bringing up her family without help.

In addition to their normal seed mixture, turquoisines should be given bread soaked in weak honey water, seeding grasses and germinated seed when they are rearing youngsters.

Feeding A staple diet for these birds should include plain canary seed, millets, oats and small quantities of hemp and sunflower. They are fond of green food and individuals may take a little fruit. Grit and cuttlefish bone must always be available.

Elegant Grass Parrakeet (*Neophema elegans*)
Southern and Western Australia

Description 230 mm (9 in.). An appropriately named little bird; although not brightly coloured it is unquestionably one of the most attractive of the grass parrakeets. Mainly olive-green in colour; forehead with a cobalt-blue band, bordered with paler blue; similar pattern on edge of wings; throat and breast greenish yellow, shading into yellow on the lower breast and abdomen. Bill grey-black; legs grey-brown.

Females are similar but the colours are rather more muted.

General Management Elegant Grass Parrakeets are generally hardy and easy to manage. They thrive in fairly small aviaries (a flight not less than 3 m (10 ft) in length will suit a pair of these birds) and are hardy enough to stay outside throughout the year. A dry and frost-free shelter should be provided, of course.

Except when breeding they are quiet, inoffensive little birds and they can be safely housed with companions.

Their aviary is best placed in a secluded though sunny spot. While they could never be described as drab or uninteresting, it is really during the spring and early summer months that they come into their own. The breeding season results in great activity, with the male performing an amusing little courtship display which includes much bobbing of the head while he sings his pleasant, rather twittering, little song.

Breeding These birds make use of boxes measuring about 250 mm (10 in.) square and 450 mm (18 in.) deep. They should be hung in a sheltered part of the flight.

Four or five eggs are laid and the female incubates for 18 to 20 days. The young birds leave the nest about a month later. Like related species, young Elegant Grass Parrakeets usually prove to be very nervous during their first few weeks out of the nest and it is mainly for this reason that a secluded site for the breeding aviary is recommended.

The young are reared without addition to their parents' staple diet.

Feeding A staple diet for these birds consists of a canary/millet mixture. They can also be given small quantities of sunflower and hemp. Plenty of green food should be supplied and they are also fond of seeding grasses. Grit and cuttlefish bone should always be available.

Red-rumped Parrakeet (*Psephotus haematonotus*)
Southern and south-eastern Australia

Description 280 mm (11 in.). Probably the best-known and most widely kept (with the exception of the budgerigar) of the Australian parrakeets. Head, breast and upper surfaces green; back dark green; rump red; underparts yellow; wings edged with dark blue. Bill black; legs grey.

Females are not as brightly coloured and lack the distinctive red rump. Bill grey.

General Management The Red-rumped Parrakeet is hardy, easily managed and a good breeder – therefore, an excellent bird for beginners.

Like related species they should be provided with a roomy aviary. Although they do not require heated quarters during the winter months a comfortable shelter should be provided for roosting purposes. Flying exercise is important for these and similar species; a flight measuring 4–5 m (12–15 ft) in length is ideal.

Although some authorities claim that red-rumps can safely be housed with other species, this is far from others' experience. Individual birds may vary a good deal in temperament, but in general terms they are not to be recommended for mixed collections.

Breeding A healthy, compatible pair of Red-rumped Parrakeets usually breed without problem and are capable of rearing up to ten chicks in the course of a season.

They need a typical parrakeet nest-box measuring about 300 mm (12 in.) square by 600 mm (24 in.) deep. About 100 mm (4 in.) of decayed wood should be provided in the box.

From four to seven eggs are laid. Incubation lasts for about 21 days and is carried out only by the female. The young birds leave the nest after about a month.

The youngsters are usually reared without the need for addition to their parents' diet. They should be left in the breeding aviary for about two or three weeks after they have left the nest, but a careful watch must be kept on the male at this time as he may attack the young birds when the female goes to nest again.

Feeding Red-rumps are very easy to feed and thrive on a mixed seed diet which includes plain canary, millets, hemp, sunflower, groats and oats. They are fond of green food and an occasional slice of apple. Grit and cuttlefish bone are essential additions to their diet.

Golden-mantled Rosella (*Platycercus eximius cecilae*)
Southern Queensland and interior of New South Wales

Description 380 mm (15 in.). A colourful Australian broadtail parrakeet which lives and breeds well in aviaries. Head, neck and upper breast bright scarlet; a conspicuous white patch extends from cheeks to throat; lower breast yellow; feathers of back and scapulars black with bright yellow borders giving a laced effect; wing and tail feathers in various shades of blue. Bill whitish horn; legs grey-black.

Females are very similar but the colours are slightly less bright.

General Management These are essentially aviary birds which should be housed in lengthy flights. They are hardy and will winter outside without difficulty. They should be provided with a shed for roosting purposes.

Although, like most other parrot-like species, they will chew at exposed pieces of timber it is unlikely they will do a great deal of damage to the aviary structure. There is little point in attempting to grow any kind of plants in their flight for these would be very quickly destroyed. Perches are best provided at each end of the flight so the birds have plenty of space for flying exercise.

In a really large aviary the floor can be of natural earth or turf. Smaller flights are best constructed with a concrete base which can be hosed down from time to time.

Breeding A healthy pair of Golden-mantled Rosellas, properly housed and fed, will usually go to nest without a great deal of fuss. They should, of course, be the sole occupants of the breeding aviary.

Nest-boxes should be placed in a shady part of the flight and can be fixed to the top of a stout tree stump to give a more natural appearance. The box itself should be about 230 mm (9 in.) square and 500 mm (20 in.) deep with an entrance hole placed fairly close to the top. Strips of wood should be nailed, ladder-fashion, inside the box so that the birds can scramble up to the hole. The box should have some kind of concave base to prevent the eggs from rolling about.

The clutch consists of from four to eight eggs. Incubation, which is carried out by the female, lasts 21 days. The chicks will be reared without the need for addition to the adult birds' staple diet.

Feeding A good staple seed mixture for these parrakeets should contain plain canary, white and yellow millets, oats, sunflower, hemp and buckwheat. In addition the birds should have regular supplies of fresh green food – chickweed, groundsel, dandelion and such like.

Most parrakeets appreciate regular supplies of fresh twigs and branches from which they will strip the bark. Branches of apple and other fruit trees are excellent; hawthorn is perhaps more easily available, and just as acceptable to the birds. Grit and cuttlefish bone must always be available.

Abyssinian Lovebird (*Agapornis taranta*) Ethiopia

Description 165 mm (6½ in.). Largest of the lovebirds and a good aviary bird, being hardy and not difficult to breed. Mainly green in colour, darkest on the head, wings and mantle; under surfaces pale green; forehead red. Bill red; legs grey.

Females are similar but lack the red forehead patch.

General Management Best housed alone in small aviaries. It is unwise to attempt to keep this species on the colony system and while non-breeding birds can be accommodated with suitable companions this can often prove to be a dangerous arrangement and the lovebirds frequently attack much larger birds without provocation.

They are hardy birds and can be housed outdoors throughout the year without heat. A comfortable shelter must be provided and efforts made to accustom the birds to using it; if food and water vessels are placed inside the shed this will usually bring about the desired result. Apart from providing shelter from the elements, a roosting shed is valuable as a refuge for these birds, which are easily startled, particularly after dark, and can inflict serious injuries upon themselves by flying headlong into the wire-netting of their flight.

Lovebirds will also roost in boxes, but this can create problems should they decide to nest out of season when the females may succumb to egg-binding.

Breeding One advantage Abyssinian Lovebirds have over many of their relatives is the ease with which they can be sexed. A true pair will usually settle down to breeding in a small compartment aviary. Either hollow logs or boxes should be provided and hung in the open part of their aviary; they should not be placed where they will be subject to the full rays of the sun.

Plenty of willow or apple twigs should be provided for nest-building. From four to six eggs are laid. Incubation lasts about 21 days and the young remain in the nest for a further five to six weeks.

The youngsters are not difficult to rear. Some aviculturists provide soaked bread or sponge cake as additional foods at this time but these appear to be largely ignored by many birds. Sprouted seeds, seeding grass heads add extra green food should be offered.

Feeding A staple diet of plain canary seed, millets, small quantities of hemp and sunflower suits these birds. They are fond of greenstuff and enjoy an occasional slice of apple. They should always have grit and cuttlefish bone.

Masked Lovebird (*Agapornis personata*)

North-eastern Tanzania

Description 140 mm (5½ in.). An extremely handsome little lovebird and one of the most popular with aviculturists. Head, cheeks and throat dull black; nape and breast yellow; wings green with some black in the flight feathers; lower under surfaces pale green; eye-ring white. Bill red; legs grey.

The sexes are alike.

General Management This is one of the most widely kept members of the family of lovebirds. Although they are sometimes kept in colonies there is a risk, as with others of the family, of young birds being attacked and injured in the nest by other members of the group. They are happy in small aviaries and single pairs in each compartment seems to be the best and safest way of breeding these birds.

Masked Lovebirds are perfectly hardy and can be wintered outside without heat. They should have a dry and frost-free shelter. While they can stand low temperatures, damp conditions are another matter entirely and must be regarded as a major health hazard.

Growing plants will not last long in any lovebird aviary. The birds will make short work of almost every type of vegetation, and furnishings should be limited to plenty of natural branches. The birds will quickly strip the bark from these, particularly when nesting, and care must be taken to see that no poisonous kinds are used. Willow is suitable as are branches from fruit trees; hawthorn can also be used.

Breeding Masked Lovebirds are easily bred. Unfortunately they are difficult to sex and many 'true' pairs eventually prove to be two birds of the same sex.

They will use either boxes or hollow logs and construct a large nest which eventually occupies most of the nesting receptacle. As with other species of lovebirds, plenty of sappy twigs and branches should be provided at this time; the moist bark is an important factor in maintaining humidity in the nest while eggs are being incubated.

Up to six eggs are laid and incubation lasts about three weeks. The youngsters are not difficult to rear but the Masked Lovebird is one of a number of the members of this family which pluck their youngsters while they are in the nest. There seems little one can do to prevent this happening, although individual pairs vary a great deal and some will cause no trouble at all.

Feeding Masked Lovebirds should have a mixed seed diet which includes plain canary seed, white and yellow millets, together with a little hemp and sunflower seed. They are fond of green food. Grit and cuttlefish bone must always be available.

Peach-faced Lovebird (*Agapornis roseicollis*) East Africa

Description 150 mm (6 in.). Handsome little birds and probably the easiest of the lovebirds to breed in confinement. Mainly apple-green in colour; under surfaces yellow-green; forehead rose-red; sides of head and throat salmon-pink; rump sky-blue. Bill yellow; legs grey. The sexes are alike.

General Management Best housed in pairs in small aviaries; Peach-faced Lovebirds are not suitable for colony-system breeding. They are hardy and, if provided with a suitable shelter, can remain outside throughout the year without heat. They like to roost in nest-boxes, but this can lead to eggs being laid out of season with a consequent risk of egg-binding.

Breeding These handsome lovebirds are free breeders. They will make use of budgie-type nest-boxes and should be supplied with plenty of natural branches from which to strip bark for nest-building. The female carries this and various other bits and pieces of material to her nest-box by tucking them into the feathers of her rump.

The supply of suitable twigs and branches must be maintained throughout the breeding season as the birds will continually add strips of bark to maintain humidity in the nesting chamber.

Feeding Peach-faced Lovebirds thrive on a diet of plain canary seed and millet, to which can be added quantities of hemp and sunflower seed. Regular supplies of green food should be provided. Grit and cuttlefish bone are essential.

Fischer's Lovebird (*Agapornis fischeri*) Northern Tanzania

Description 140 mm (5½ in.). A popular species with aviculturists for many years. Hardy, easy to house, feed and breed it is an excellent bird for novices. Mainly grass-green in colour; forehead bright red; rest of head, face, neck and breast orange-red with a faint olive-green suffusion. Bill red; legs grey.

The sexes are alike.

General Management A pair of Fischer's Lovebirds will thrive in a small outdoor aviary. Alternatively, several pairs can be housed together in more spacious quarters. They live well in colonies but breeding results are unlikely to be as good as those achieved with individual pairs housed in small compartments.

They are hardy and do not require heat during winter, but must have comfortable, dry, sleeping accommodation.

Breeding Nest-boxes similar to those provided for budgerigars suit these birds. They should be provided with suitable branches from which they will strip the bark to produce essential humidity in the nest-box.

Young lovebirds are reared without addition to the adults' normal diet.

Feeding A good staple diet consists of equal parts of plain canary seed and mixed millets. They should also be given smaller quantities of hemp and sunflower seed. They enjoy green food, fruit and an occasional millet spray. Grit and cuttlefish bone should always be available.

Plum-headed Parrakeet (*Psittacula cyanocephala*)
India and Ceylon

Description 355 mm (14 in.). One of the most beautiful parrakeets which thrive in aviaries. Upper surfaces green; breast and underparts yellowish green; head rose-pink; throat and collar black; shoulder patch dark red; some blue and yellow feathers in wings and tail. Bill orange-red; legs grey.

Females are similar but have a blue-grey head and lack the red shoulder patches. Bill yellow.

General Management Such beautiful, easily managed and adaptable birds are a good choice among the parrot tribe.

Newly acquired birds are sometimes difficult to wean on to a mixed seed diet, seeming to prefer an intake of millet only. This, of course, is not adequate and efforts must be made to persuade them to take a more varied menu.

When acclimatised they can be housed outdoors throughout the year. A shelter should be provided for roosting. An aviary to house these birds does not need to be very large, although they are such graceful birds that a lengthy flight will enable them to display themselves to advantage.

They are usually tolerant of other birds and can, if necessary, be housed with some of the larger seedeaters or other parrot-like species with an amiable disposition.

Plum-heads are not noisy birds; in fact the male's call-note during the breeding season is extremely musical.

Breeding A pair of Plum-heads must have an aviary to themselves if it is hoped to breed from them. They are not particularly free breeders – nor are females as freely available as their more brightly coloured mates. Many 'true' pairs eventually prove to be two males; young males are almost identical to adult females.

Nest-boxes should be about 250 mm (10 in.) square and between 600 and 900 mm (24 and 36 in.) deep. Some decayed wood or coarse sawdust should be placed in the bottom to a depth of about 50 mm (2 in.).

Although nest-boxes should be hung up in the flight section of the aviary, they should have some protection from the elements – including strong sunshine.

Incubation of up to six eggs is carried out by the female. The breeding pair must be disturbed as little as possible; Plum-heads are shy breeders and eggs are likely to be abandoned if the breeding pair are subject to any undue interference.

Extra food should be provided when youngsters are in the nest and this can include soaked bread as well as additional green food.

Feeding A seed diet which includes canary, millets, sunflower, ground-nuts and a little hemp suits these birds well. They like green food and apple. Grit must always be available.

African Grey Parrot (*Psittacus erithacus*)
Equatorial Africa

Description 355 mm (14 in.). One of the most familiar members of the parrot family. Widely kept as a household pet and valued for its ability to mimic the human voice. Entire plumage silvery grey, paler on the under surfaces; tail and under tail coverts bright red. Bill black; legs dark grey.

The sexes are alike.

General Management The majority of African Grey Parrots are condemned to spend the whole of their lives in tiny parrot cages – hardly big enough to allow a budgerigar sufficient exercise, let alone a bird of this size. Caged parrots should be allowed out of their cages for exercise as often as possible.

A garden aviary to house a pair of these birds should be built of chain-link or welded mesh netting on a heavy-duty metal frame. Any bare wood will quickly be reduced to shavings by the birds' powerful beaks. Remember that they can give a nasty bite and should be handled with care.

Breeding African Greys have bred only on rare occassions in aviaries. A pair should be given a substantial wooden nest-box or barrel. It may be several years before they decide to go to nest. The two to four eggs take about a month to hatch and the young remain in the nest for a further two to three months.

Feeding A good staple diet for these birds includes sunflower, hemp, ground-nuts, buckwheat and plain canary. They should have regular supplies of green food and fruit. Grit must be offered.

Senegal Parrot (*Poicephalus senegalus*) West Africa
Yellow-bellied Senegal Parrot, Yellow-vented Senegal Parrot

Description 250 mm (10 in.). Attractive little African parrots. Hand-reared birds make wonderful pets. Head and throat dark grey; rest of upper surfaces bright green; lower breast and abdomen yellow-orange. Bill silvery horn with black tip; legs black.

The sexes are alike, although males usually prove to have heavier bills than their mates.

General Management Senegal Parrots are admirable aviary birds and will live for years in a suitable flight. They share their larger relatives' ability to destroy all but the most substantial woodwork and their aviary is best constructed with a metal framework. They are hardy but should have a shelter for use during severe weather.

Breeding Few breeding successes have been recorded with this species – a little disappointing in view of the large numbers available.

A breeding pair will make use of a stout nest-box or hollow log. Two eggs are laid and the chicks are reared without addition to the adult birds' normal diet.

Feeding Senegal Parrots are very easy to feed. They thrive on a mixed seed diet which includes plain canary, millets, sunflower and some ground-nuts. They are fond of green food and fruit. Grit should always be available for them.

Canary-winged Parrakeet (*Brotogeris versicolurus*)
Tropical South America

Description 230 mm (9 in.). Attractive little parrakeets which are kept widely as pets. Young birds settle down quickly and usually become tame and confiding. Mainly grass-green in colour; under surfaces with a faint yellowish wash; conspicuous yellow patch in wings; area of bare skin around eye pale blue. Bill dark yellow; legs grey.

The sexes are alike.

General Management Many of these birds are obtained as house pets and although young birds usually adapt fairly quickly to the sort of domestic routine more usually associated with budgerigars, adults are a different proposition and rarely settle down in a small cage. They become hardy and can be housed outdoors throughout the year. They should have a dry shelter but do not require heated quarters when they are acclimatised.

Like most members of the parrot family they are not suitable occupants for a planted aviary and their flight should be furnished with an assortment of stout branches. They appreciate a hollow log or stout wooden box in which to roost, and newly acquired birds which have not settled down will often retire to the privacy of their box when danger – either real or imagined – threatens.

The Canary-winged Parrakeets are attractive birds in most respects, but they have loud and rather penetrating voices which may upset neighbours who do not share an interest in birds.

Breeding A true pair of Canary-winged Parrakeets can be persuaded to breed in a suitable aviary. They will probably prefer a hollow log as a nesting receptacle, although boxes are also used.

Up to six eggs are laid and incubation lasts for 22 to 24 days. The chicks remain in the nest for a further seven to eight weeks. The youngsters are usually reared without the need for additions to their parents' diet.

Feeding A mixture of plain canary seed, white and yellow millets, small quantities of hemp, sunflower and buckwheat. They also need regular supplies of green food – groundsel, shepherd's purse, etc. – and fruit. They must always have supplies of grit and cuttlefish bone.

Quaker Parrakeet (*Myiopsitta monachus*)

Bolivia, Paraguay, Uruguay and Argentina

Grey-breasted Parrakeet, Monk Parrakeet

Description 280 mm (11 in.). Interesting birds which build communal nests. Best housed in large aviaries, or at liberty. Forehead and breast grey; feathers of breast edged with pale grey; upper surfaces green; some blue in wing feathers. Bill flesh-coloured; legs grey. The sexes are alike.

General Management These are not really birds for the suburban aviary. Apart from their unusual nesting habits they are also extremely noisy and their strident voices will hardly endear them (or their owner) to neighbours.

A small colony can be housed in a spacious outdoor aviary where they will usually start to construct their enormous nest during late spring. Once incubation gets under way it is possible to open the aviary and let the birds fly free. In a suitable environment it is perfectly feasible to establish a permanent free-flying colony – using the aviary, perhaps, as a feeding station.

They are extremely hardy birds and usually prove well able to stand up to the vagaries of a mild winter.

Before attempts are made to establish a free-flying colony of Quaker Parrakeets it should be borne in mind that they can do considerable damage to ornamental trees and shrubs; during the spring they are likely to make short work of buds and young shoots.

Breeding Quaker Parrakeets are not difficult to breed either at liberty or in a suitable aviary. Two or three pairs in a roomy flight will quickly construct a bulky nest, making use of twigs, small branches and various fibrous materials.

The young are easily reared and it is not necessary to add to the parents' normal diet If the adults are at liberty they will collect a variety of natural foods on which to feed their brood. Incidentally, the nest serves as a roosting area as well as providing compartments for incubation and rearing of young.

Feeding A good-quality parrakeet mixture suits these birds. It should include plain canary seed, some hemp and sunflower, buckwheat, white and yellow millets. They are fond of green food and fruit.

Grit and cuttlefish bone should always be available, although liberty birds will usually ignore these last two items.

Cockatiel (*Nymphicus hollandicus*) Australia
Cockatoo-Parrot

Description 330 mm (13 in.). Handsome birds with a fine, upstanding crest. Live and breed well in aviaries. Upper surfaces grey; underparts light grey with a faint tinge of yellow-buff; front of head, crest, cheeks and throat bright yellow; ear coverts orange; conspicuous area of white down centre of wing. Bill and legs dark grey.

The female is similar but the yellow areas on her face and throat are less bright. The underside of the female's tail is barred with yellow and grey.

General Management With the exception of the budgerigar, probably the best known and most widely kept member of the parrot family. Cockatiels are excellent subjects for the beginner. Easy to house, feed and breed, they will give the novice valuable experience before tackling more delicate species.

A breeding pair should have an aviary to themselves to ensure success. Despite their size, they are surprisingly gentle birds and, when not breeding, can be housed with most other compatible species, including small finches.

Cockatiels are strong flyers. They are at their best in a lengthy flight which provides opportunity for plenty of wing exercise. While they are perfectly hardy, a shelter should be provided for protection against severe winter weather.

Breeding Cockatiels are extremely prolific and a healthy pair can usually be relied on to produce three broods during a season. Since up to six or more eggs are laid to a clutch it will be apparent that this is one of the few species of parrot-like birds which increases its aviary-bred stock so rapidly.

A pair of Cockatiels should be provided with a large wooden nest-box hung in a sheltered part of the flight. Sawdust or decayed wood should be placed in the bottom.

Although they are free breeders in aviaries they will rarely tolerate disturbance once nesting operations are under way.

The parents will rear their brood without addition to their normal diet, although some sprouted seeds and seeding grass heads will be appreciated.

Feeding A diet of plain canary seed, white and yellow millets suits these birds. They can also be given a little hemp and sunflower seed. Fresh green food should be given. Cockatiels also enjoy such fruit as apple. Grit and cuttlefish bone is essential at all times.

Lesser Sulphur-crested Cockatoo (*Kakatoe sulphurea*)

Celebes

Description 355 mm (14 in.). A widely kept species, although most often as a domestic 'pet' and not as an aviary bird. Mainly white, with a faint yellowish wash; cheek patches pale yellow; crest bright lemon-yellow. Bill and legs grey-black.

The sexes are very similar but can be distinguished by the colours of their eyes; the male's iris is almost black while that of the female is brown.

General Management These cockatoos are small enough to be accommodated in an aviary of quite modest dimensions. Like their larger relatives, however, they will make short work of exposed timbers, and accommodation should be metal-framed. Heavy-duty netting is also desirable.

They are totally unsuitable for planted aviaries, but their quarters should be furnished with plenty of natural branches. These will need to be replaced at frequent intervals as the birds dismember them.

This is a hardy species which can be housed outside throughout the year. Although they do not require heat, a dry shelter is essential.

Like many related species, the Lesser Sulphur-crested Cockatoo is an intelligent bird and some become quite talented talkers. It has to be emphasised, however, that birds which have been kept as pets for long periods are rarely of value as potential breeding stock.

Breeding Although by no means a frequent occurrence, this species has been bred in aviaries. An established and compatible breeding pair will make use of a stoutly built box or barrel, or a hollow log of suitable dimensions.

Two or three eggs are laid. Incubation appears to be shared by both sexes; the eggs hatch after about four weeks but it is a further two months before the youngsters leave the nest. In addition to their normal diet, the parents should be given egg food, germinated seed and extra green food.

Feeding A standard parrot mixture consisting of sunflower seed, hemp, ground-nuts, plain canary seed, buckwheat, etc. suits these birds well. Green food should be offered regularly together with fruit (they are fond of a slice of apple), green vegetables and carrots. They should also have a supply of grit.

Yellow-backed Lory (*Domicella garrula flavopalliata*)
Moluccas

Description 290 mm (11½ in.). A brilliantly coloured lory which makes a good aviary subject. Infrequently available. Plumage mainly crimson; wings green with prominent area of yellow on wing butts; shoulders and upper back yellow; tail with black tip. Bill orange-red; legs grey.

The sexes are alike.

General Management When acclimatised, Yellow-backed Lories are excellent aviary occupants. They become hardy and can be kept outdoors throughout the year. A frost-free shelter should be provided and the birds usually prefer to sleep in a box or hollow log.

They are not suitable subjects for cages or indoor flights. When closely confined their quarters must be maintained in a scrupulously clean condition. In an aviary they usually prove to be enthusiastic bathers and keep themselves in excellent feather as a result.

Like most related species they are not trustworthy with other birds and a pair must have an aviary to themselves. They often form close attachments with their owner and can prove extremely endearing and amusing pets.

Breeding Lories are by no means the easiest avicultural subjects to breed from. But they are well worth persevering with.

They should have as large an aviary as possible. Part of the top can be covered with rigid polythene to provide shelter from driving rain and strong winds. Although these birds become hardy, climatic extremes can cause problems unless precautions are taken to provide them with a measure of protection.

Either hollow logs or nest-boxes should be provided. They should be fixed in position in a secluded part of the outside flight. The usual clutch consists of two eggs which hatch after an incubation period of nearly a month. The youngsters do not emerge from the nest for a further three to four months, at which point they are extremely well developed.

The young birds are usually reared without addition to their parents' diet.

It is highly desirable to fit special perforated metal bases to nest-boxes or logs being used by these birds. Their droppings are naturally liquid and copious, and taking into account also the long period of time in which the young occupy the nesting receptacle it will be seen that a precaution of this kind is almost essential.

Feeding These birds should have a varied diet consisting of sponge cake soaked in an artificial nectar mixture, various fruits and some seeds, although the last may be ignored.

Purple-capped Lory (*Domicella domicella*)
Assam and Amboyna

Description 300 mm (12 in.). Back and underparts deep red with orange band across the upper breast; crown black at front merging into deep purple at the back; wings predominantly green with yellow webs to flights; thighs and small patch on the bend of the wing blue; tail mainly deep red with purple band near the tip. Bill orange; legs black.

General Management When acclimatised, these birds do well in an outside aviary but require a frost-proof shelter during the winter months. Ideally a little heat should be provided in really cold weather.

The soft food necessary for these birds causes their excreta to be very wet and it is essential, therefore, to keep their surroundings scrupulously clean. These birds soon settle down to aviary life, becoming quite tame.

Breeding A garden aviary is ideal for breeding, and pairs should be housed alone. They should be provided with a hollow log or box. Usually two eggs are laid; the female undertakes incubation, hatching occurring in 25 days.

Feeding Purple-capped Lories need a diet of sponge cake soaked in artificial nectar mixture, together with a variety of soft fruits. They should also have some boiled rice and some seed including plain canary and millets, but will not thrive on an all-seed diet.

Meyer's Lorikeet (*Psitteuteles flavoviridis meyeri*)
Celebes

Description 215 mm (8½ in.). Attractive little Lorikeets which are not often available. They do well in garden aviaries but appear not to be completely hardy. Mainly green in colour; forehead pale apple-green; nape olive-green; under surfaces yellow-green – the feathers having darker edges. Bill orange-red; legs grey.

The sexes are alike.

General Management Attractively coloured but lacking the flamboyance of other members of the family, Meyer's Lorikeets need care until they are acclimatised. They can be housed in an outdoor aviary throughout the year but should have a slightly warmed shelter for use during the colder months; alternatively they can spend the winter in roomy indoor flights. Their aviary should have at least one-third of the flight covered with polythene to provide protection from winds and rain.

Breeding Neither Meyer's Lorikeet nor related species are easy to breed. They may make use of a hollow log or a suitable box. Up to four eggs are laid and incubation lasts for approximately three weeks. The young birds remain in the nest for a further six weeks after hatching.

If the adult birds are correctly fed it will not be necessary to provide other foods when youngsters are being reared.

Feeding Meyer's Lorikeets need a varied diet which includes sponge cake soaked in honey water or an artificial nectar mixture, various fruits – including apples, pears, grapes, etc. – and a seed mixture; the latter can include plain canary seed and millets.

Swainson's Lorikeet (*Trichoglossus haematodus moluccanus*)

Eastern and south-eastern Australia

Blue-mountain Lorikeet, Rainbow Lorikeet

Description 300 mm (12 in.). A brilliantly coloured nectar-feeding parrot which well merits its alternative name – Rainbow Lorikeet. Back, wings and tail bright grass-green; head, throat and lower breast bright purplish blue; nape yellowish; breast orange-red. Bill orange; legs grey.

The sexes are identical.

General Management When acclimatised they can be housed outside throughout the year. Adequate shelter should always be available, and during the coldest months of the year slight heat is advisable.

Space and cleanliness are two essential factors in the successful care and management of these and related species. Their droppings are naturally liquid and copious; in a small aviary plumage quickly becomes soiled and the birds' general health and well-being suffer as a consequence.

Lorikeets are delightfully playful and a pair will tumble and wrestle like kittens. Unfortunately they are also somewhat given to produce shrill and ear-piercing calls – which may not be appreciated by neighbours.

Breeding Swainson's Lorikeets have been bred on numerous occasions and there are many records of successful hybridisation with closely related sub-species. There is little to be gained from such cross-breeding and it is important that aviary-bred stocks of these and many other species are kept pure.

A roomy wooden nest-box or hollow log should be provided. Two eggs are laid and incubation, which lasts about a month, appears to be undertaken only by the female. The young lorikeets leave the nest about seven or eight weeks later.

The adults make use of their staple diet to feed the chicks but should have additional supplies of sponge cake soaked in honey water and some sprouted seeds at this time.

Feeding These birds are rather 'messy' feeders. They will often almost dive into a dish of soft fruit or soaked sponge cake while feeding – which is one reason they bathe so frequently!

A good-quality sponge cake soaked in honey water or one of the proprietary nectar mixtures suits them well. Plenty of soft fruit is also needed – grapes, pears, chopped apples, etc. Their seed mixture should include plain canary seed, millets, a little hemp and sunflower. Green food should be offered, together with some live food.

Red Lory (*Eos borneus*) Moluccas

Description 380 mm (15 in.). Vividly coloured birds which are available rather infrequently. Some blue in wings and under tail coverts; flight feathers black; tail orange; the remainder of the plumage deep scarlet. Bill red; legs black.

The sexes are alike.

General Management This magnificent lory is available in fairly small numbers and is much sought after by parrot specialists.

When first obtained they should be housed in spacious indoor quarters. Remember that, like most parrot-like species, they are capable of undertaking a speedy and efficient demolition job on flimsy wooden cages or aviaries. A flight to accommodate a pair of these birds should have a metal framework supporting heavy-gauge wire-netting.

Their droppings are liquid and copious – since they feed mainly on fruit and nectar mixtures. Their accommodation must be maintained in a scrupulously clean condition or the birds' plumage – and almost certainly their general health – will suffer.

These lories should not be associated with other birds in either cages or aviaries. They can be exceedingly savage and are capable of unprovoked attacks on other birds which usually end in serious injury or death for the victim. On the other hand they usually become very tame and form close attachments with their owner.

Breeding Few lories have been bred with any marked degree of regularity in controlled conditions. Success is more likely if they are given permanent quarters for occupation throughout the year. Many of these birds take time to settle down and it may be the second or third year before they show any inclination to go to nest.

One or two large, hollow tree stumps are valuable furnishings in an aviary housing a pair of these birds. These will be used for roosting as well as nesting purposes. Although lories will make use of boxes a more natural-looking receptacle may make for more successful breeding results.

Two eggs are laid. After hatching, the chicks remain in the nest for several weeks and are fed by both parents throughout this time. The adult birds' normal diet is adequate for rearing purposes.

Feeding Lories are brush-tongued and in the wild feed to a great extent on nectar and soft fruits. In aviaries they are given an artificial nectar mixture to which is added some plain sponge cake. Some aviculturists give them sweetened bread and milk but this can be a risky practice, particularly during the summer months when the mixture is likely to go sour very quickly.

Pears, grapes, sweet oranges, apples, etc. should all be included in the diet for these birds. A parrakeet seed mixture can also be provided.

Zebra Dove (*Geopelia striata*) Malaysia

Barred Ground Dove

Description 230 mm (9 in.). Charming little birds for a secluded garden aviary, not quite as hardy or easy to manage as the closely related Diamond Dove. Head and throat grey – with a pinkish wash on the back of the head and nape; back and upper surfaces brown; sides of neck and breast finely barred with black and white; centre of breast vinous-fawn shading to off-white on the abdomen. Bill dark grey; legs red-brown.

The sexes are virtually identical, although females are usually more slightly built.

General Management Zebra Doves are frequently available and should be treated in much the same way as Diamond Doves. Although they become hardy, newly acquired birds should be carefully acclimatised before they are housed out of doors. They can eventually remain outside throughout the year but are best confined in a frost-free shelter during the worst months of the winter.

They are never really at home in a bare or sparsely planted flight and their aviary should contain adequate cover. They can share quarters with other birds (not other doves or pigeons) but their nervousness can often result in wholesale panic in a mixed flight.

Breeding Like other members of the family, Zebra Doves construct an extremely flimsy nest and it is better to try to persuade them to make use of a shallow box or basket. Left to their own devices, Zebra Doves usually lay their eggs on a fragile platform of twigs placed across the fork of a shrub. A small piece of wire-netting can sometimes be slid into place under the 'nest' to prevent its collapse, but this is a difficult operation, for the parents will abandon their eggs without a great deal of provocation.

The young birds are usually reared without difficulty. They usually leave the nest after a couple of weeks and their parents will continue to feed them for a few days before starting on a second brood. The first brood must be removed as soon as their parents show signs of going to nest again.

Feeding Zebra Doves require little other than a mixture of plain canary seed, white and yellow millets. They like maw seed and also enjoy items of green food. Like other members of the family they swallow seeds and grain without removing the husk. Grit, important for all seedeating species, is a vital digestive aid for these birds.

Diamond Dove (*Geopelia cuneata*) Australia

Description 190 (7½ in.). These tiny doves should find a place in every collection of foreign birds. Hardy and easy to feed, they breed freely in aviaries. Most of the plumage is soft blue-grey; wings and tail grey-brown; abdomen white; wings spotted with white; circle of bare skin around eye red. Bill black; legs flesh-coloured.

The sexes are similar but, in breeding condition, the male's eye-ring is larger and brighter.

General Management These pretty little doves are very popular aviary subjects. Unlike many of the smaller members of the pigeon family, Diamond Doves are hardy and can be housed outside throughout the year provided they have dry sleeping quarters. Efforts should be made to persuade these birds to roost inside a shelter. They are sometimes inclined to take fright (particularly after dark) when danger – either real or imagined – threatens. Apart from the very real possibility of damaging themselves they can also cause wholesale panic among companions. In an enclosed shelter these difficulties are less likely to arise.

Diamond Doves are excellent companions for any other birds which will not molest them. They can be safely housed with waxbills and other small seedeaters. Unfortunately they are completely intolerant of other doves and attempts to keep more than one pair in the same aviary will lead to serious fighting.

In most respects they are ideal aviary birds. Easy to house, feed and breed, their gentle call-notes lack the monotony of some of the larger doves and pigeons.

Whilst the typical grey form is by far the most popular and widely kept, there is also a handsome silver mutation available.

Breeding Diamond Doves usually make use of nest pans or shallow boxes in which to lay their two eggs. Incubation lasts 15 days and the young leave the nest about two weeks later. They are reared without addition to their parents' diet.

Not more than three or four broods per season should be taken from the breeding pair.

Feeding Mixed millets and some plain canary seed will provide a good staple diet for these little doves. They enjoy maw seed and also like to pick over a wild seed mixture. Green food should be given. Grit is essential.

Chinese Painted Quail (*Excalfactoria chinensis*) Southern Asia
Blue-breasted Quail, Button Quail

Description 130 mm (5 in.). A delightful miniature game bird which lives and breeds well in an outdoor aviary. Upper surfaces brown, mottled with black and with lighter striations; cheeks, chin and throat patterned in black and white; breast and flanks blue-grey; rest of underparts bright chestnut. Bill black; legs yellow.

Females are predominantly brown with darker barrings on the breast.

General Management These diminutive game birds are ideal companions for any species which will not molest them.

They should be provided with plenty of ground cover in their aviary. Tussocks of grass are much appreciated and usually provide the chosen nest site.

Breeding Eight or more eggs are laid in a shallow depression hidden in long grass. The chicks hatch after 16 days and are able to run about as soon as they are dry. It is essential the aviary has a board surround for the chicks are small enough to get through even 12 mm ($\frac{1}{2}$ in.) mesh netting. They should be fed on insectile food, maw seed and very small maggots and the like. The chicks should be removed to another aviary when about four weeks old.

Feeding The basic diet should consist of various millets and plain canary seed; they are also fond of maw seed. Plenty of greenstuff should be provided together with items of live food. The latter must be rationed during the winter months or the female may be induced to lay out of season. Grit must be available at all times.

Californian Quail (*Lophortyx californicus*) Western USA

Description 250 mm (10 in.). An attractive ground-dwelling bird for the aviary. Mainly grey in colour with handsome black and white markings on face and throat; lower breast buff, the feathers edged with buff giving a scaly appearance; similar patterning on feathers of nape and sides of neck; white streaks on flanks; black club-shaped crest. Bill and legs black. Females lack the black and white markings on face and throat. They have a shorter crest of brown feathers.

General Management Hardy and easily managed, they need a spacious aviary with plenty of ground cover. Ample dry shelter accommodation should be provided.

They like to roost high and perches should be fixed in position in secluded parts of the aviary. Californian Quail are rather prone to night frights and roosting spots need to be screened with bunches of spruce or other evergreens.

Breeding Californian Quail are prolific breeders and the females will often lay 20 or more eggs. They are somewhat less reliable when it comes to incubating.

Eggs can be hatched under a bantam or in an incubator. The chicks should be given either a fine-grade insectile mixture or canary rearing food with some maw seed and small maggots. Chopped green food should be added.

Young quail grow quickly and are self-supporting in a matter of weeks. The sexes are best separated as soon as they can be distinguished.

Feeding Basic diet consists of seeds and small grain. They also need green food and some live food. Grit is essential.

Species Index